MUSCLECAR
COLOR • HISTORY

# CHEVELLE
## 1964-1972

Mike Mueller

MBI Publishing Company

First published in 1993 by MBI
Publishing Company,
PO Box 1, 729 Prospect Avenue,
Osceola, WI 54020-0001 USA

MBI Publishing Company books are
also available at discounts in bulk
quantity for industrial or sales-
promotional use. For details write to
Special Sales Manager at
Motorbooks International
Wholesalers & Distributors,
729 Prospect Avenue, PO Box 1,
Osceola, WI 54020-0001 USA

Library of Congress Cataloging-in-
Publication Data

Mueller, Mike.
    Chevelle 1964–1972 / Mike
    Mueller.
        p.   cm.—(MBI Publishing
        Company muscle car color
        history)
    Includes index.
    ISBN 0-87938-761-0
    1. Chevelle automobile—History.
        I. Title    II. Series.
    TL215.C48M85   1993
    629.222'2—dc20          93-13164

*On the front cover:* Chevelle muscle
is dressed in red, black, and chrome
in this 1966 L78 (375hp) SS 396
owned by Bob and Christa Gatchel,
Clermont, Florida.

*On the frontispiece;* The L78
engine: 396ci producing 375hp.

*On the title page:* Among the final
wave of true muscle cars was this
Mulsanne Blue 1971 Chevelle SS
convertible owned by Jack Hunter,
Boca Raton, Florida.

*On the back cover:* The last of its
breed, a 1972 LS5 454 Chevelle SS
owned by Mike and Judi Murphy,
Delray Beach, Florida.

Printed in Hong Kong

# Contents

# Acknowledgments

Honestly speaking, I've never owned an SS Chevelle, not one. I was too young when they first prowled the streets, I was too poor once I came of age, and now I'm too married. Had I rearranged a few things in my life—obligations, responsibilities, finances—there's no doubt in my mind that at some time or another I would have parked at least one SS 396 in my garage, or maybe just down by the curb. I may still. Chevrolet's Super Sport legacy has impressed this writer since high school, when everyone seemed to have a Chevelle—except me.

Perhaps that's why I jumped at the opportunity to put together a Super Sport Chevelle book. A respect for history, a love for the cars, and a reasonable tolerance for writing seemed just the ticket to make up for all those years of not driving one of Detroit's all-time most popular muscle cars. While some might say my not having lived up close and personal with at least one qualifies me as being unqualified to tell the Chevelle SS tale, I beg to differ. On the contrary, not being so close allowed me to step back and take a good long look. This is a practice commonly overlooked by those who would just as soon praise the car of their dreams at all costs, instead of telling history like it was, or as close to it was as one could expect from a perspective of twenty to thirty years down the road.

Without a doubt, these were great cars—perhaps the greatest of the muscle car era as far as general popularity is concerned. In base form, the SS 396 was affordable, exciting, and every bit the muscle car as anything else on the market in those days. Yet there were chinks, making Chevrolet's big-block Chevelles not unlike anything else around. Chevy's first SS 396, the 1965 Z16, was certainly a helluva performance machine, but it was also a high-priced promotional piece few could touch. On the other hand, the 1966 SS 396 cost nearly $1,500 less, but offered an almost equal fraction of the Z16's performance and pizzazz.

Clearly, the common denominator was cost. By 1968, any buyer could have outfitted himself in a truly hot car if he had the money. Options, if you could afford them, cured all ills. But the controlling factor most often considered by the average customer, who couldn't carry the financing weight of a fully loaded model nor juggle the need for practical transportation with a desire for playful performance, was getting the most bang for the buck. A car that worked hard, held up well, perhaps looked good, and ran like the wind, all for a price a working guy could handle, that was the kind of factory hot rod that appealed to the greatest group of buyers. Performance for the masses? Although many automakers tried to capture this market, when you consider Chevrolet was selling nearly 90,000 Super Sports at the top of the sixties roller coaster, you find yourself wondering if anyone ever did it any better.

You tell me.

Although this book may not be stuffed full of rosy recounts and lavish embellishments, it is jam-packed with Chevelles: great, not-so-great, and otherwise. Numbers alone define popularity, and seemingly nothing has changed since my days in high school when almost every guy was driving an SS 396. Demonstrated photographically on these pages is my attempt to parade before you as many of the different varieties, year by year, as possible.

Through it all, I hope I've produced not a pep rally but a history, a history from which you can draw your own conclusions.

Pulling this history together required the assistance of friends and strangers alike. By the time this is through, perhaps those strangers will be friends as well. First, a tip of the hat goes to Mark Broderick at Chevrolet Public Relations for coming through when it counted despite an avalanche of demands on his end. Hooking up with automotive historian Terry Boyce at the last minute added to this project as well. And where would I be without the enthusiasm of Mark Meekins of the National Chevelle Owners Association in Greensboro, North Carolina, a learned and very busy man who never once failed to drop everything and answer my questions over the phone.

Also helping burn up my phone and fax lines were Mick Price and Roger Gibson. A Yenko collector and devoted Chevy man, Mick not only let me and my Hasselblad into his little shop on the prairie, he also did his darndest to make sure I got my Yenko facts right. The same goes for Roger, who opened the doors of his world-class restoration shop in Kelso, Missouri, and not only educated me on Yenkos and COPOs, but also rolled out Fred Knoop's glorious 1969 427 Chevelle for a complete photo shoot. Thanks, guys. See you again soon on my next whirlwind tour through the Midwest.

And the list goes on. Both my good friends Ray Quinlan in Champaign, Illinois, and Jack Hunter down in Boca Raton, Florida, helped find photogenic feature cars. Will Fox and Mitch Frumkin at Publications International in Chicago, and fellow Motorbooks author Tony Young up the road near Orlando, came through with some valuable historical photos, as did my good buddies John Mauk, at the Daytona Racing Archives in Daytona Beach, and Skip Norman, of Gold Dust Classics in Ashland, Virginia. Additional appreciation goes to Scott Gaulter in the Des Moines area for helping with my chapters on 1964 and 1965, and to Chevelle nut Jeff Dotterer of Kempton, Pennsylvania, for his assistance in locating feature subjects.

Meanwhile, here in Lakeland, Florida, *Chevy Action* editor Jason Scott managed to separate himself from his grindstone just long enough to discuss a few details and supply a clue or two. And local writer/photographer Rob Reaser put his nose to the wheel in order to meet a withering succession of film-developing and print-making deadlines, all in the best interest of filling his pockets with my cash. But seriously, without Rob's sweat and encouragement I'd still be begging my editors in Stillwater, Minnesota, for yet another deadline extension.

Of course, I couldn't get away without at least mentioning my brother David's name; without his able assistance and "unquenchable" camaraderie during countless photo shoots throughout the Midwest last summer, I probably would be exactly where I am right now—but I wouldn't have had near as much fun getting here. Also of honorable mention is my wife Denise, who held down the fort with nary a whimper while I went on various photographic rampages. And I must give credit where credit is due to Jim Mueller, my dad, for working so hard over the years to teach me as much about cars—and maybe a little about life—as is humanly possible, whether I wanted to learn or not.

Finally, special thanks surely go to all the car owners who donated their time to making this book happen, sharing their prized possessions with me and you. Their cooperation, patience, and hospitality are greatly appreciated. Although I would love to offer befitting gratitude to these men and women individually, there are only so many pages available here. Following is a list of these people and their cars in a basic order of appearance in this book:

Don Allen, Winter Haven, Florida, 1955 Bel Air; Marty Locke, Lucasville, Ohio, 1961 409 Impala SS; Scott Gaulter, Waukee, Iowa, 1964 L76 Chevelle SS; Bob Dykstra, of Ageless Autos, Zeeland, Michigan, 1964 Chevelle SS convertible; Frank Ristagno, Philadelphia, Pennsylvania, 1964 409 Impala SS convertible; Floyd Garrett, Fernandina Beach, Florida, 1965 Z16; Charlie Stinson, Mt. Dora, Florida, 1965 Chevelle SS convertible; Bill Worthington, Apopka, Florida, 1965 L79 El Camino; Bruce Clem, Clearwater, Florida, 1966 SS 396 (blue); Bob Gatchel, Clermont, Florida, 1966 SS 396 (red); Sam Pierce, Anderson, Indiana, 1967 SS 396; Rusty Symmes, Winchester, Indiana, 1968 SS 396; Gary Place, Homer, Illinois, 1969 L78 SS 396, 1969 Yenko Chevelle (gold), and 1972 SS big-block hardtop; Gary Adkins, Dresden, Tennessee, 1969 L89 SS 396 300 Deluxe; Fred Knoop, Atherton, Georgia, 1969 COPO 427 Chevelle; Mick Price, Atwood, Illinois, 1969 Yenko Chevelle (green); Randall and Patti Fort, New Smyrna Beach, Florida, 1970 SS 454 (red); David and Dusty Fox, Ft. Myers, Florida, 1970 SS 396; Carl Beck, Clearwater, Florida, 1970 SS 396 El Camino; Lukason and Son Collection, Florida, 1970 LS6 convertible; Russ Werley, Hamburg, Pennsylvania, 1971 SS convertible (red); Jack Hunter, Boca Raton, Florida, 1971 SS convertible (blue); Ed and Diann Kuziel, Tampa, Florida, 1971 SS 454; Bonnie and Mike Smith, Hollywood, Florida, 1972 SS convertible (red); Mike and Judi Murphy, Delray Beach, Florida, 1972 SS 454 convertible.

A gracious thank you to everyone—let's do it again sometime.

# Chapter 1

# Introduction

## *Bow-Tie Bloodlines*

In the early sixties, there was a major gap between the top and bottom in
Chevy's ranks. It was clear a new car could be built to fill that gap.
That new 'A-body' car was to be a larger, full-framed model to replace the unit-body
senior compacts. Chevrolet's A-body would emerge as the Chevelle.

Detroit's muscle car era basically came to an end some twenty years ago. By 1971, automakers had begun reversing power levels and squeezing compression ratios in an effort to reduce emissions per government mandates. Some said environment-minded legislators were expecting too much, while others claimed the picture wasn't as bleak as it was painted; solutions, as many clean air crusaders demanded, could not be brought about overnight.

Nevertheless, the plug was yanked on factory horsepower almost before you could say "parts per billion." Skyrocketing insurance rates and safety-conscious Congressmen would have brought about the same end had Detroit not been forced to clean up its act. Accordingly, most legendary boulevard brutes were gone by 1972,

*Opposite*
*Easily the most popular among Chevelle Super Sports, the 1970 model represented the pinnacle of Chevrolet's mid-sized muscle development. Few rivals could catch them—and, as this famous promotional photo reveals, the only true way to stop the 1970 Chevelle SS in optional SS 454 trim was to tie it down.*

*In 1955, Chevrolet introduced low-priced performance. Armed with Chevrolet's new overhead-valve V-8, the 1955 Chevy did indeed steal the thunder from the higher-priced crowd, and gave birth to a performance legacy that continues running strong to this day.*

leaving only a few tamed survivors to carry on the tradition until, a few years later, they too faded away.

Among these were Chevrolet's Super Sport Chevelles. In their time, they didn't come much more popular, whether in early small-block, proven SS 396, dominating SS 454, or later "mouse-motor" forms. Numbers said it all; from 1964 to 1972, Chevrolet built more than 525,000 V-8 Super Sport Chevelles (six-cylinder models were available in 1964 and 1965).

Big-blocks were clearly the cars to have, but you didn't necessarily need to own an SS 396 to be in with the in crowd. Even if your Chevelle were powered only by the lowly 307ci small-block, you were still a member of the fraternity—certainly the slowest of the lot, but a member nonetheless. Even then there was hope, knowing how easily a mouse motor responded to a little warming over. Interchangeability made Chevy's small-block one of the most versatile powerplants of its day—or any other, for that matter. Parts were plentiful (junkyards were stuffed full), power options were varied (mixing and matching was no problem), and the sky was basically the limit (how fast depended only on how much you wanted to spend).

Demonstrating that brawn wasn't Chevelle's only selling point, total sport coupe and convertible production surpassed 2.2 million through 1972. And the car's proven popularity among younger buyers didn't die once emissions controls took over. Well into the eighties, Chevelles—SS 396, SS 454, or small-block—still dominated high school parking lots everywhere you looked, rivaled perhaps only by their Camaro cousins.

Explaining Chevelle popularity is simple enough. Considering all the car had to offer, including its "U.S.A. 1" heritage, how could it lose? Performance potential, sporty good looks, reasonable roominess in an easy-to-handle size—all this and more helped make Chevelles major drawing cards

*Opposite*
*Nine years later, the Chevelle picked up where the "Hot One" left off.*

*Chevy's Hot One grew even hotter in 1956, thanks to twenty-five more horses under the hood. Here, on September 9, 1955, Zora Arkus-Duntov races up Pikes Peak in a camouflaged 1956 Chevrolet, on his way to slicing two minutes off the American stock sedan record. Later in the year, the 225hp, dual-carb Corvette V-8 was made an option for the 1956 Chevy.*

from day one. And then there was the Bow-Tie legacy.

Once Chevelles started making the rounds in 1964, members of the automotive press couldn't resist comparing them to the "Hot One," the legendary 1955 Chevy, and rightly so. The cars were quite similar in size and looks—clearly, designers reached back for a few proven quantities to give an all-new model line a boost out of the blocks.

Of course, filling the Hot One's shoes was no easy task. Featuring Chevrolet's first modern overhead valve V-8, Ed Cole's baby had pushed aside the company's tired "Stovebolt" image. With the optional 180hp Power Pak and 4.11:1 gears, a 1955 Chevy was the hottest thing going, able to

| **Success Side By Side** | | |
|---|---|---|
| | **1955 Bel Air Sport Coupe** | **1964 Chevelle Sport Coupe** |
| Wheelbase | 115in | 115in |
| Length | 195.6in | 193.9in |
| Width | 74.0in | 74.6in |
| Height | 62.1in | 54.5in |
| Weight | 3,195lb | 3,390lb |
| Horsepower | 162• | 195* |
| | •base 265ci V-8 | *base 283ci V-8 |

*Vince Piggins joined Chevrolet in 1956, after helping make the Hudson Hornets NASCAR kings in the early fifties. Piggins would become one of Chevrolet's most active performance proponents. He died on October 17, 1985.*

"out-accelerate any American car on the market today!" according to *Road & Track*. But just when Detroit watchers had thought they'd seen it all, the Hot One got even hotter for 1956.

The year began with Zora Arkus-Duntov dashing up Pikes Peak in a camouflaged 1956 Bel Air, shattering the existing American stock sedan record by slightly more than two minutes. Powering Duntov's Bel Air was the new 205hp Super Turbo-Fire 265 V-8, the engine that inspired *Mechanix Illustrated* writer Tom McCahill to label the 1956 Chevy the "best performance buy in the world"—and that was before Chevrolet began offering the 225hp Corvette V-8 under passenger-car hoods.

The Corvette 265, introduced midyear, featured twin four-barrel carburetors, a solid-lifter cam, and 9.25:1 compression. McCahill described the offering as "a poor man's answer to a hot Ferrari," then topped his earlier boast, claiming the 225hp 265 V-8 "might very well be rated the greatest competition engine ever

built." Proof of McCahill's claim wasn't hard to find.

In 1955, Chevys had captured the National Association of Stock Car Auto Racing's (NASCAR) short track division, thanks primarily to Daytona Beach speed merchant Smokey Yunick. Yunick and driver Herb Thomas had been lured away from Hudson, which had dominated NASCAR competition from 1952 to 1954. Thomas was the topflight driver Ed Cole wanted to help put Chevrolet in the forefront on the track, and Yunick was simply the best damn mechanic in town. It was no small wonder Chevrolet picked up the pace in 1956, winning in both Short Track competition and the newly formed Convertible division.

Through Yunick's urging, Chevrolet hired Vince Piggins in 1956. A Hudson refugee as well, Piggins had been Yunick's engineering contact during the successful "Fabulous Hornet" years. At Chevrolet, Piggins began a long career of overseeing the company's performance projects, especially those that could be put to good use at the track.

Chevrolet continued winning at the track in 1957, partly because of a little clever manipulation by General Motors head Harlow "Red" Curtice. At a meeting of the Automobile Manufacturers Association (AMA) in February 1957, Curtice proposed a ban of sorts on factory racing involvement, supposedly to prevent automakers from competing with their customers. AMA action earlier that year had already banned fuel injection and superchargers—high-powered options introduced by Chevrolet and Ford, respectively—from NASCAR competition. On the surface, Curtice's proposal seemed in keeping with this effort to put a lid on Detroit's burgeoning horsepower race

*Chevrolet first introduced the Super Sport package as an Impala option in mid-1961. Featuring "knockoff" wheel covers, splashy trim, and sporty interior treatments, the Impala SS was basically intended to showcase the hot new 409 V-8, which was a Super Sport option. Standard SS power came from the 409's forefather, the 348, an engine first designed for truck duty in 1958.*

in the interest of fair play at the track. Besides, the move was financially smart; racing was expensive, a conclusion to which Ford chief Robert McNamara could relate. McNamara agreed with Curtice, and the infamous AMA "ban" on factory racing involvement was instituted in June.

But while McNamara took Ford completely out of the race, GM simply went underground, giving Pontiac and Chevrolet an edge they wouldn't relinquish until Henry Ford II officially denounced the AMA ban in June 1962. As for NASCAR competition immediately following the ban, Chevy swept through all three divisions in the second half of the 1957 season, taking top honors in Grand National, Convertible, and Short Track racing.

Even though Smokey Yunick switched his allegiance to Pontiac's Semon E. "Bunkie" Knudsen the following year, the Bow-Tie legacy continued in powerful fashion. Chevrolets had grown in size considerably by 1958, and the hot little small-block was no longer up to the task of throwing all that weight around. Replacement came in the form of an engine originally designed for truck duty, the "W-head" 348, the first in a long line of potent Chevy big-block V-8s. In top triple-carb trim, the 348 remained Chevy's number one powerplant through 1960.

Then came 1961. Big news for the year came in two forms. The first went into production in January and almost immediately took National Hot Rod Association (NHRA) drag strips by storm. Derived from the yeoman 348, the famed 409 V-8 was a drag racing demon right out of the crate. The sec-

*Super Sport status was extended down to compact ranks in 1963 for the Chevy II Nova, although six-cylinder power was as hot as it got. An optional V-8 would appear the following year.*

ond form was introduced shortly thereafter. Created to help showcase the 409, the Super Sport kit added a classy dose of performance imagery. On the outside, special trim and spinner hubcaps caught the eye. Inside, a passenger-side grab bar on the dash, a 7000rpm tachometer, and a mini-console floor plate for four-speed cars heightened the Super Sport's exclusivity. Power steering and brakes, sintered metallic brake linings, and heavy-duty suspension completed the package.

Yet another newsworthy event occurred in November 1961, when Bunkie Knudsen moved over from Pontiac to Chevrolet, eventually bringing Smokey Yunick's expertise back into the Chevy camp as well. With performance-minded Knudsen as general manager, Piggins pulling the engineering strings, and Yunick working behind the scenes on the racetrack end of the deal, there appeared to be no limits to what Chevrolet would unleash. Supporting this belief were the Z11 409 and the Mark II "Mystery Motor," both created in 1962.

Although each displaced 427ci, the two racing mills were as different as night and day. Developed in late 1962, the Z11 was a stroked 409. Built with super stock drag racing in mind, the 430hp Z11s went into 1963 Chevys with aluminum front ends. About fifty-five were built. Later, a handful of Z11s turned up under the hoods of factory-experimental 1964 Chevelle drag cars.

The Mk II 427, however, never was made available, going into only five specially prepared Grand National stockers for competition in the 1963 Daytona 500. Created by engineer Dick Keinath in July 1962, the Mk II resembled the Z11 only slightly in the bottom end. On top, the Mk II's "porcupine" canted-valve heads represented a marked improvement over the old W-head 348-409 design. Reportedly, the Mk II dynoed at about 520hp. At

Daytona, that power translated into record performances during qualifying, but various difficulties left the five Mystery Motor Chevys in the dust as Fords copped the top five places. All that, of course, came about in February 1963.

One month before, on January 21, GM corporate officials had determined they'd seen enough, passing the word from the fourteenth floor down to all divisions to cease and desist race-related activities. The Z11 project was nipped in the bud, while the Mk II made its mysterious appearance at Daytona and then disappeared back into the shadows. Apparently, the front office felt results weren't worth the investment. Negative publicity was also a factor, as automotive safety concerns had just started taking real root. And besides, GM had other, more important projects to concentrate on.

General Motors was heavily involved in new model line development at the time. Multiple model lines still represented an unproven approach in 1963, with full-sized models existing as the standard line while compacts filled in as economical alternatives. Chevrolet's ground-breaking Corvair had appeared in 1959, followed in 1961 by what were then referred to as senior compacts, Buick's Special and Oldsmobile's F-85. A purely practical budget buggy placed one notch above the Corvair when introduced in 1962, Chevrolet's little Chevy II gained a tad more pizzazz and prestige once Super Sport imagery was applied in 1963.

What remained was a major gap between top and bottom in Chevy's ranks. Although the terms "intermediate" or "mid-sized" had yet to be coined, it was clear a new car could be built to fill that gap. In GM terms, that new car was to be an "A-body," a larger, full-framed model to replace the unit-body senior compacts.

Chevrolet's A-body would emerge as the Chevelle.

# Chapter 2

# 1964

## *Plugging the Gap*

"Last week Chevrolet General Manager S. E. ('Bunkie') Knudsen showed to
the press the auto that is expected to do the job: the new Chevelle. Impressed by its
clean and handsome styling, Detroit's normally undemonstrative auto reporters
broke into spontaneous applause."

—*Time* Magazine, August 30, 1963

**B**y 1963 the grapevine was ripe with rumor and fact alike concerning General Motor's upcoming A-bodies, which would be put to use in 1964 by the B-O-P triumvirate (Buick, Oldsmobile, and Pontiac) as well as by Chevrolet. For Buick, Olds, and Pontiac, the A-body would become the enlarged home for the existing Special, F-85, and Tempest, respectively. On the other hand, the application would represent an entirely new approach for Chevrolet.

Accordingly, the automotive press spilled a lot of ink attempting to hang a label on the all-new Chevy. Of next to no help were Chevrolet officials who seemingly weren't even sure

*Opposite*
*Curved side glance, exceptionally clean sheet metal, and clear family ties to the ground-breaking 1955 models were the calling cards of the new 1964 Chevelle. While dimensions were similar to those of the 1955 Chevy, the flat, lattice-work grille up front was obviously a takeoff on the 1964 full-sized design. Crossflag emblem on fender signifies the optional 327ci V-8, in this case the mysterious 365hp L76 Corvette V-8, installed by the car's owner to depict what one of these ultra-rare A-bodies would look like.*

*From the rear, the 1964 Chevelle's boxy lines and "scalloped" rear wheel openings best demonstrate the car's ties to Chevy's "Hot One" of nine years before. Along with special emblems, Super Sport exterior treatment included eye-catching "SS" wheel covers, as well as brightwork topping off the upper body edge and running around the wheel openings, along the rocker panels, and behind the rear wheels. Super Sport equipment tacked on another $162 to the asking price for a 1964 Malibu hardtop or convertible.*

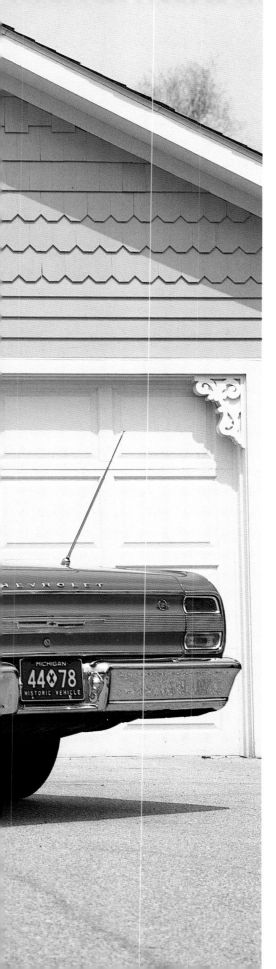

what they had. Formed in clay by March 1962, Chevy's A-body image went through more than one identity crisis before its final transformation into sheet metal. One clay of April 1962 clearly resembled an upsized Chevy II, a design decision that would have fallen in line with those planned by the B-O-P clan. A family resemblance to the smaller Chevy was a common theme in the studio throughout the styling process. Then, adding to the confusion, a January 1963 mock-up carried "Chevy II Nova" identification.

*Car Life* first made mention of these "bigger little cars" in its February 1963 issue. "It looks strongly at this point as though some of the compact cars for '64 will be even bigger and longer," read *Car Life*'s report, "in which case they'll hardly qualify as compacts." It noted a resized Chevy II right along with Buick's Special, Oldsmobile's F-85, and Pontiac's Tempest. All four reportedly were to share a new perimeter-frame chassis with a 114in wheelbase. At the time, the B-O-P trio had a 112in unit-body chassis, while the unitized Chevy II's wheelbase was 2in shorter.

*Motor Trend* made a similar reference two months later, announcing GM's plans for an enlarged Chevy II to share the same body of the B-O-P cars. Also mentioned was the switch to perimeter-frame construction. According to *Motor Trend*, GM engineers had "never been satisfied with unit construction on their compacts" because of difficulties in minimizing road rumble, rattles, and shakes. With the A-bodies being larger and heavier, that job would become even tougher. Restyling limitations inherent with unit body design were given as other

*Out of 76,860 Super Sport Chevelles produced for 1964, 11,191 were convertibles—1,551 with six-cylinders; 9,640 with V-8s. The "V" emblem on the front fender of this 1964 droptop SS announces the presence of the 283ci small-block. Popularity of Super Sport Chevelle convertibles never again matched that of the 1964 model. The wheel covers on this 1964 SS convertible are incorrect— they're 1963 Impala Super Sport units (which 1963 SS Novas used as well).*

good reasons to slide a frame under the new cars.

As *Car Life*'s Roger Huntington later explained, "the more expensive and complex tooling required for unit bodies prevented [GM stylists] from making the deep annual styling changes that are such an important part of the 'dynamic obsolescence' philosophy used by GM. Another factor is that the general shape of panels for unit bodies has an effect on the overall structural strength. This also puts a damper on stylists' ideas. There is no such limitation with frame bodies."

In actuality, the frame that engineers had in mind for the A-body ended up rolling on a 115in wheelbase with coil springs at all four corners. And yes, the guys upstairs had initially planned on ending the little Chevy II's life, with the thinking being that another new model line would serve only to eat into Chevrolet's already established four-tiered sales structure. But by the end of February 1963, the decision was made to add another model line, and in late April, "Malibu" made its first appearance on an A-body mock-up.

Interestingly, a piece of conceptual line art labelled "Chevy II" appeared in *Motor Trend*'s August 1963 issue. "Indications are very strong that Chevrolet will modify the current Chevy II, making it wider and longer," explained the report, "[and the car] might get a new name in the bargain." Bingo. Reappearing in the September edition, the identical artwork was renamed "1964 Chevelle." "Chevelle, if that's what it's called, will bear family resemblances to the big one and the Chevy II," predicted *Motor Trend*.

Official news of the transformation appeared earlier in that same issue. "There'll be a 1964 Chevy II, contrary to some reports," began the notice. "Originally, word was that Chevrolet's new compact car (called in some quarters the Chevair), using the new GM 'A' body, would replace the Chevy II. Then we heard the new car would be called the Chevy II, though it would have an entirely different chassis and body. The current Chevy II was to be phased out. Now, latest word is production of the Chevy II will be continued."

Reason given was that the "new Chevair design" ended up being pricier

19

## CHEVELLE IS THE CAR

## THAT'S MADE BY THE PEOPLE

**WHO MAKE THE CORVAIR AND CORVETTE**—Meet the Chevelle Malibu Super Sport. Chevelle is Chevrolet's dapper new package—115-inch wheelbase, separate perimeter-type frame, supple Full Coil suspension, and crisp, tasteful styling. Malibu Super Sport is the series, very strong on elegance, that charges Chevelle with a flavor you can trace right back to the Corvair and Corvette. In a word, sporting. It includes bucket front seats, all-vinyl interior trim, special instrumentation (oil and water temperature gauges and ammeter), and Super Sport wheel disks, trim and identification. Chevelle's performance options* include all-synchro 4-speed shift, Positraction and sintered-metallic brakes. And a 283-cubic-inch 220-hp V8 with 4-barrel carburetion and dual exhausts. Malibu Super Sports come in Coupe or Convertible versions. Both seem like sports cars until you start piling people and luggage into them. . . . Chevrolet Division of General Motors, Detroit, Michigan.

*Optional at extra cost

**CHEVROLET**

*Previous pages*
*Resemblances between Chevrolet's 1964 Impala and the new Chevelle were evident in both overall lines and the cars' front ends, each featuring lattice grilles and minimal overhang.*

*Still lacking a true performance image, Chevrolet's Chevelle Super Sport was played up in 1964 as being "sporting." Offered as a six-cylinder in base form and initially going only as high as 220hp with the optional L77 283ci V-8, SS Chevelles were certainly no match for their GTO counterparts from Pontiac.*

than planned, putting it too close to the full-sized Chevy and too far from the affordable Corvair. There was still a definite niche for the Chevy II, which had sold well in 1963, and suddenly Chevrolet recognized a need to "blanket the market." In the end, like it or not, Chevrolet general manager Bunkie Knudsen found himself presiding over five distinct model lines for 1964.

"Intermediate" became the accepted handle for the new Chevelle not long after the decision to offer five model lines was made. In an October 1963 report explaining how GM's A-body prototypes were tipping the scales more aggressively than predicted, *Motor Trend* used the term at will: "For all practical purposes, these new 'intermediates' are the size and weight of a 1955 Chevrolet." Putting two and two together, *Motor Trend* then went on to predict that the A-body intermediates would "eventually replace some of the GM full-sized car lines," a thought echoed by Roger Huntington, who still wasn't quite sure how to describe the new Chevelle. "It isn't really a compact," he wrote in *Car Life*'s October 1963 issue, "so we wouldn't be surprised if the full-size Chevrolet is completely phased out within two years, in favor of this slightly smaller car."

Both magazines reported Chevrolet's decision to allot fifteen percent of its September production run to the Chevelle line, a decision that somehow lead Huntington to conclude that Chevy officials had "big plans for this new size of car." At that point, all that remained was the coming out party.

Knudsen took care of that before a gathered throng in late August, introducing the all-new 1964 Chevelle to rave reviews. *Time* magazine told the tale in its August 30, 1963, issue: "Though its sales are already greater than those of the entire Ford Motor Company, Chevrolet has for 1964 prepared a whole new line of intermediate models in an effort to win more sales. Last week Chevrolet General Manager S. E. ('Bunkie') Knudsen showed to the press the auto that is expected to do the job: the new Chevelle. Impressed by its clean and handsome styling, Detroit's normally undemonstrative auto reporters broke into spontaneous applause." Without a doubt, Chevy designers had put their collective finger directly on the pulse.

Looks were the key. Clean and uncluttered, although boxy, the new body was quite a departure from what had come before. Almost. Much could be said—and was—concerning the 1964 Chevelle's general resemblance to the "Hot One" itself.

"Somehow, we couldn't help feeling we'd driven the Chevelle before, about eight years ago," wrote *Motor Trend*'s Bob McVay. "It's basically very similar to the popular 1955 Chevrolet—a shade shorter in overall length and height, but with the same basic engine-chassis combination." Along with its comparable stature, the Chevelle's squared-off ends, slab-side sheet metal, and "scalloped" rear wheel openings easily represented modern variations on the 1955 theme.

But heredity wasn't the only apparent influence. Those boxy lines and squared-off nose and tail also helped the 1964 Chevelle pass for a downsized 1964 Impala. The resemblance was especially evident up front, where the quad headlights and lattice grille, rounded at both ends, showed definite full-sized family ties. Copied or not, the look was described by Chevy's ad crew as "all new, already classic!" A bit more restrained, *Car Life* felt the Chevelle stood "among the most handsome of the 1964 automobiles, providing the too-busy 'dual-cove' rear styling treatment is overlooked."

*Motorcade* wasn't quite so forgiving, pointing a thumbs down in the direction of the new Chevelle because of its truncated profile. Unlike its B-O-P A-body counterparts, the Chevelle had 10in taken from its rear overhang. According to *Motorcade*, "this makes for a lighter and more compact car—but it doesn't do anything for looks. The Chevelle looks stubby and ill-proportioned with a wheelbase of 115 in and overall length of 193 in." Luckily, buyers weren't quite as critical.

One month after Knudsen's party, *Automotive News* reported that "the only complaint about Chevelle was that dealers couldn't get enough of them." After three months, Chevelle was the second-hottest selling Chevy, taking up eighteen percent of Chevro-

Chevrolet general manager Semon E. "Bunkie" Knudsen (at podium to left) introduces the all-new Chevelle, in Super Sport garb, of course, to the press in August 1963. Initial responses bordered on raves.

let's production schedule. By the time the smoke had cleared, model year production (discounting El Camino) had reached 338,286—some 60,000 above Ford's Fairlane, and tops in the intermediate ranks.

Nearly twenty-three percent of that total was made up by Chevelle Super Sports, available in Malibu hardtop or convertible form, powered both by six-cylinders and V-8s. In keeping with tradition, Chevelle's Super Sport package offered most of the things that had been making the Impala SS so appealing since 1961, and the little Nova SS since 1963. Included, of course, were bucket seats, a console with floor shifter for Powerglide and four-speed equipped Super Sports, a deluxe sport steering wheel, SS badging, and distinctive SS wheelcovers. A slightly different brightwork arrangement on the outside set an SS apart from a standard Malibu, and a four-gauge cluster (temperature, ammeter, oil, and fuel) replaced the base Chevelle's idiot lights.

Popular performance options included a tachometer in place of the

clock (which moved to a pod on the dash), metallic brake linings, heavy-duty suspension, heavy-duty clutch, larger four-ply tires up to 7.50x14, a Positraction differential, and 3.36:1 "special purpose or mountain" rear gears (3.08:1 gears were standard). Overall, the Chevelle SS image was attractive, as 76,860 customers apparently agreed.

From a true performance perspective, Chevelle's beginnings were humble at best. Even for the sporty SS, standard power came from a 120hp 194ci six-cylinder, with the optional 155hp 230ci six-cylinder (Regular Production Order, or RPO, number L61) waiting in the wings. But the Chevelle SS, by definition, wasn't the type of car you'd expect to be pulled around by a six-cylinder, and accordingly only 9,775 were sold for 1964.

Doing the right thing, more than 67,000 buyers chose the V-8 models, which in base form were powered by a 195hp 283ci small-block. To allow the 283 entrance into the A-body platform, the tried-and-true "ram's horns" exhaust manifolds, with their center dumps, were replaced by redesigned manifolds exiting to the rear.

The strongest powertrain option initially presented to Chevelle cus- tomers was RPO L77, a 283 small-block specifically prepared for the A-body application. At 9.25:1 compression, the L77 was identical to the 195hp 283, but rated at 220hp thanks primarily to the addition of a Rochester four-barrel carburetor, a re-curved distributor, and dual exhausts. When mated to the optional Muncie M20 four-speed, the L77 small-block made a valiant attempt to put the Super in Super Sport.

*Motor Trend*'s McVay liked the L77 for its hop-up performance potential. "In its 220-hp Chevelle form, it was quiet, willing, and reliable," he wrote. "But more importantly," he continued, the L77 "is an engine that lends itself well to the owner who wants more than the 220hp offered by Chevrolet." McVay's tests of an L77 four-speed 1964 Super Sport produced a 9.7-second 0-60 run and a quarter-mile time of 17.4 seconds at 80mph.

Doing *Motor Trend* one better, *Car and Driver*'s testers described the L77's response as "volcanic," although they admitted some credit had to belong to the new Muncie four-speed, built at GM's plant in Muncie, Indiana. Replacing the T-10 four-speed manual previously purchased from

*Demonstrating that early A-body Super Sports featured more show than go was the fact that customers could have equipped their SS Chevelles with six-cylinders for both 1964 and 1965. Standard six-cylinder fare in 1964 was the truly weak 120hp 194ci variety, with this version—RPO L61, the 155hp 230ci High-Thrift Six—waiting in the wings. Chevrolet sold 9,775 six-cylinder Super Sports in 1964; 8,585 in 1965.*

Borg-Warner, the M20 was a marked improvement. According to *Car and Driver*, the Muncie gearbox was "light and quick, and certainly one of the very best transmissions now on the market." Apparently relying on a heavier foot, the *Car and Driver* crew managed 0-60 in 8.5 seconds, and 16.6 seconds in the quarter-mile.

Among *Car Life*'s conclusions was a smoother shift, thanks to the "robust" Muncie four-speed. "Because of a more rigid bracket assembly, shifts have a somewhat tighter feel than the T-10 unit but are quicker, positive and a wrist-flick apart." Flicking his wrist with abandon, *Car Life*'s test flogger scored the best run in a 220hp Chevelle, turning a 16.2-second quarter-mile and topping out at 84mph. Rest to 60mph took 8.7 seconds.

Fully synchronized, the M20 featured wider gears to handle higher torque loads, and specially designed teeth to reduce noise. Its synchronizers, bearings, and output shaft were all beefed to handle anything thrown at it by a performance powerplant. Representing a good start for the Chevelle's performance legacy, the Muncie gearbox was the only real choice for performance-minded buyers who couldn't bear the thought of being shackled to the sluggish two-speed Powerglide automatic. In its March 1964 report, *Car Life* detailed the need for a "well-designed, modern three-speed automatic" in the Chevelle, but that was still to come.

In the meantime, engineers upped the horsepower ante, thanks to a little in-house competition. Despite overriding pressures from the GM braintrust to keep a lid on performance, Elliot "Pete" Estes over at Pontiac had managed to let the 389-powered GTO slip past corporate sticks-in-the-mud, leaving the new Chevelle in the dust and forcing Bunkie Knudsen's hand.

Although Chevrolet didn't have a big-block V-8 comparable to Pontiac's 389 available for the Chevelle in late 1963 (the aging 409 wasn't compatible and the "Mark motors" were still mysteries), it did have the small-block 327, the Corvette's heart and soul. In December 1963, Chevrolet announced two 327s—RPOs L30 and L74—as Chevelle options. Rated at 250 and 300hp, respectively, both had 10.5:1

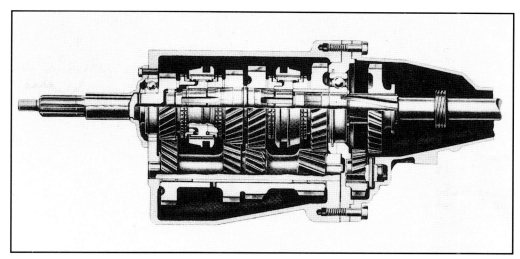

*Perhaps the most prominent performance offering presented to Chevelle SS buyers in 1964 was the equally new Muncie four-speed manual transmission, a beefed-up gearbox capable of handling whatever the* Chevy small-block V-8 could put out. Car and Driver *called the M20 four-speed "one of the very best transmissions now on the market."*

compression and four-barrel carburetors. Entering production in March 1964, the L30 327 eventually attracted 6,598 buyers; the L74, following three months later, totalled only 1,737 units.

Chevrolet also announced an honest-to-goodness Corvette V-8, the 365hp L76 327. Not for the meek, this smoking small-block featured 11:1 compression, a "special performance" cam, and solid lifters. Had it made it to the street in any numbers, the L76 Chevelle would have been more than a match for its GTO cousin—rumor had it a factory prototype ran 0-60 in six seconds. But it was not to be.

Mentioned initially in *Motor Trend*'s March 1964 issue, the L76 was first listed in a Chevelle assembly manual dated January 27, 1964. According to *Motor Trend*, use of the L76 327 wasn't initially considered because "this sort of wild performance option in light compact cars was supposed to be taboo under GM's anti-racing policy." But once Pete Estes gained a foothold with the GTO, Chevrolet had to respond, and the Corvette-powered Chevelle was the only choice.

Chevrolet built at least one prototype, but regular production was delayed indefinitely. As *Motor Trend* warned, "don't hold your breath until you can buy a new Chevelle with a 365-hp Corvette engine. Chevrolet jumped the gun a little on the an-

nouncement of the '327' Corvette option for the Chevelle." A counter to Pontiac's publicity push was the reason given for rushing an empty promise.

The production delay involved two factors. First, 327s weren't readily available for the Chevelle application due to "unexpected demand from the big-car line." Second, exhaust manifolds compatible with the Chevelle chassis were also unavailable at the time. Apparently, the 250hp 327 could use the redesigned 283 manifolds, allowing it to fit the Chevelle chassis. "You can order this one right away," claimed *Motor Trend*. "But the 300-hp and 365-hp '327s' need bigger passages, and it's estimated that these manifolds won't be ready for assembly-line installation until May." This explains why the L74 didn't enter production until June, although engineers must have given up on the plan for larger manifolds—apparently none were ever cast—and let the higher-performance 327s hit the streets with the standard exhausts.

As for the L76, it was cancelled April 7, 1964, according to factory paperwork. The obstacles put before it, the least of which was the exhaust manifold hang-up, were apparently determined to be too great. Corporate disapproval surely must have played a part as well. Not many real hard facts are presently known about the myste-

Although Chevrolet was publicly "out of racing," thanks to GM's anti-performance edict of January 1963, it wasn't uncommon for various performance pieces to "slip out the backdoor" of Chevy's Engineering department. An early example of this was the 427 Z11 lightweight Chevelle that began campaigning early in the summer of 1964. Driven by, among others, Dick Harrell, Malcolm Durham, Jim Hays, and Neil Smith, these cars featured fiberglass body parts and lightened chassis, and turned in quarter-mile times in the high 11-second range at about 125mph.

rious 365hp 1964 Chevelle, although it is clear a few did manage to escape before the curtain came down—all prototypes, perhaps? Mark Meekins, head of the National Chevelle Owners Association, knows of one documented L76 SS hardtop, and can point to a 1964 Chevrolet publicity film showing an L76 SS convertible. It is also known that a few "backdoor" L76 factory experimental drag cars were built.

Interestingly, a specially prepared El Camino, intended to promote the 300hp 327, made the rounds among the automotive magazines in the summer of 1964. According to *Hot Rod's* Ray Brock, this custom-built test bed was originally put together with a 365hp 327 under its hood, "but after test drives, was refitted with the 300hp version." Once Brock demonstrated how wild 300 horses could be when tied to the El Camino's nose-heavy 58.3/41.7 weight bias, it was no wonder the 365hp L76 had been removed, probably before someone got hurt. As it was, totally untrustworthy traction limited the L74 El Camino to a 15.9/87 quarter-mile pass—respectable, but not nearly indicative of the L74's potential. Serious tire spin and all, 60mph went by in a mere 7.7 seconds.

Even as all this went on, rumors were circulating about the coming of a truly terrifying Chevelle powered by a descendant of the 427 "Mystery Motor," the Mark II V-8 that had turned so many heads at Daytona in 1963. Initial reports claimed a Mark motor Chevelle would appear late in 1964, but, like the three-speed automatic, that one too would have to wait.

The forerunner of a long-running performance bloodline, the 1964 Chevelle is often overlooked today. Lacking a big-block V-8 like its more aggressive A-body cousin from Pontiac, Chevrolet's new intermediate dazzled

Standard V-8 for the 1964 Chevelle SS was the 195hp 283, a direct descendant of the 265ci small-block that had made the 1955 Chevy so hot. One step up—and originally the most powerful powertrain option available for the 1964 Super Sport— was the 220hp 283, RPO L77. Total 1964 A-body production with the L77 283 was 54,840.

more with its brilliance than impressed with its muscle. Then again, that Bow-Tie bloodline had to begin somewhere. Laying the base for future performance developments, the Chevelle clearly faced nothing but sky ahead. But before it could join the super car ranks, Chevelle had to find its market niche. As *Car and Driver* explained, "with a $10 Corvair/Chevy II gap, and a $320 Chevy II/Chevrolet gap, something else was needed as a stopper. We must say, Chevelle is one of the best looking gap-pluggers we've ever seen."

And that was a start.

*Below*
*Per Chevrolet's Super Sport tradition, classy interior appointments were standard equipment for the 1964 Chevelle SS. Vinyl bucket seats, deluxe steering wheel, special instrumentation, "Malibu SS" identification, plush carpeting, and a console with floor-shifter at least made you feel like you were driving a fast car.*

*Early in the 1964 model run, Chevrolet upped the Chevelle's output ante by introducing the larger 327ci small-block V-8 into the lineup. Three versions were initially offered: the 250hp L30; the 300hp L74; and the brutish 365hp L76 Corvette 327. Featuring solid-lifters, 11:1 aluminum pistons, and an aluminum intake, the L76 would have made the Chevelle SS a real GTO killer, but the option was cancelled before it could go into true production. No one is sure how many L76 Super Sports were built—probably no more than a handful—and the few that did escape the factory may well have been developmental prototypes.*

# Chapter 3

# 1965

## *From A to Z*

"There's nothing in this world, Charlie, like slipping down the turnpike being belted in the back by 375 horsepower and in the ear by 4-speaker Bach-power!"
—Tom McCahill, *Mechanix Illustrated*

Chevrolet's A-body rolled on into 1965 appearing much like it did in 1964. A cleaner grille, various trim tricks, and larger taillights made up the most noticeable changes. Up front, a new wraparound bumper with a more pronounced "point" helped add 2.5in in length, while chassis refinements lowered the car nearly an inch. The 1965 image was more rakish overall, even though those same boxy Chevelle lines prevailed.

Super Sports carried on in similar fashion as well, still equipped with a thrifty six-cylinder in basic form. Standard power for V-8 Super Sports remained the same 195hp 283 small-block used in 1964. Meanwhile, RPO L77—the 220hp 283—was initially replaced on the options list by the 250hp

*Opposite*
*Big A-body news for 1965 came midyear in the form of RPO Z16—Chevrolet's first SS 396 Chevelle. Along with 375 horses-worth of Mk IV big-block V-8 under the hood, the Z16 Chevelle featured special exterior treatment, including this "Malibu SS 396" badge on the rear deck lid. Revised taillight trim and deleted deck lid mouldings, combined with a blacked-out cove panel, also distinguished the 1965 Z16's rear view.*

*Although the bodyshell remained the same, a "pointed" nose and revised grille / bumper design freshened the 1965 A-body's look considerably. And save for "SS" nomenclature and the limited-edition Z16 big-block option, everything that made the*

*1965 Chevelle Super Sport sporty was also available as an El Camino option. This 1965 El Camino is powered by the top small-block V-8 power choice, RPO L79, the 350hp 327.*

L30 327, although some factory literature indicated that the L77 returned in February. Whatever the case, 220hp 283s didn't show up in 1965 production records but L30s did, going into 36,261 1965 Chevelles and El Caminos.

Tops in the powertrain pecking order in the fall of 1964 was the L74 327, the 300hp variety that had thoroughly impressed *Hot Rod*'s Ray Brock under a 1964 El Camino hood earlier that summer. Featuring a large, aluminum four-barrel, dual exhausts, and 10.5:1 compression, the L74 offered ample oomph, and apparently 13,593

*Restyled standard SS wheel covers and the addition of engine identification emblems to the front fender crossflags made up the list of new Super Sport features for 1965. Wheels remained identical to those used in 1964, measuring 14x5in. RPO P67, 6.95x14 whitewall tires, was a popular option. Super Sport buyers in 1965 could either stick with the standard Chevelle SS wheelcover or opt for RPO P02, the simulated wire wheelcovers seen on the 1965 El Camino on these pages.*

customers were equally impressed. Even with the L74, however, Chevelle owners found themselves trailing the newly formed muscle car crowd as Pontiac's GTO sped away, boasting of more cubic inches and greater horsepower.

Chevrolet's first attempt to put the Chevelle into the street performance race came shortly after the new 1965 models were introduced, and again, as in 1964, involved a Corvette 327 V-8, only this time the offering wasn't a false promise. RPO L79, the optional 350hp 327, represented a valiant effort to make the Chevelle "more competitive in the booming GTO market," as *Motor Trend* explained.

The self-proclaimed muscle car progenitor, Pontiac's GTO represented the biggest target to shoot at, even among corporate cousins, a point made clear in L79 Chevelle advertisements. "The perfect squelch," was the label ads gave the 350hp Chevelle. "That's a potent squelch to all those others who keep talking about lions, tigers and such," continued the pitch, aiming the tiger reference squarely at the GTO.

*Although slightly revised in style, Super Sport exterior identification remained where it had appeared in 1964: on both rear quarters and to the right of the deck lid. Production of V-8-powered Super Sport convertibles in 1965 reached 7,995 (1,133 six-cylinder models were also built).*

One of Chevy's strongest carbureted small-blocks, the L79 relied on a Holley four-barrel, big-valve heads, and 11:1 compression to produce more than one horsepower per cubic inch, as well as 360ft-lbs of torque—this using domesticated hydraulic lifters. Armed with a 3.70:1 rear end and the requisite Muncie four-speed with its 2.56:1 low gear, a 350hp 1965 Chevelle might have surprised a GTO or two if traction were true.

Wheel spin *was* a major stumbling block, however, as *Cars* magazine's Gordon Chittenden discovered. As much as two seconds could be lost "trying to get out of the hole," he claimed. Once the tire smoke had cleared, the *Cars* crew recorded a 7.6 second 0-60 time and a quarter-mile pass of six-

teen flat—not exactly earth-shattering, but promising given the car's off-the-line handicap. Recognizing this, Chittenden concluded that "it's hard to believe Chevy's out of racing," making a reference to GM's January 1963 edict that had supposedly put a lid on high-powered, extracurricular activity.

Thanks to that edict, Chevrolet kept the wraps on the Chevelle early on, unlike Pontiac, which unleashed its 389ci GTO despite a 330ci limit GM

*The El Camino idea had been revived in 1964 as a Chevelle-based model after first appearing in full-sized fashion for 1959 and 1960. From 1964 to 1967, the Custom El Camino could be equipped with everything available to an SS Chevelle customer save for the various Super Sport trim and appearances pieces. A buyer ordering a bucket seat interior also received the SS-style wheelcovers, or he could check off RPO P02 and get the popular simulated wire wheelcovers. As replacements for the SS-type units with the bucket seat option, RPO P02 cost $57.05; if ordered with the standard bench seat, the wire wheelcovers were priced at $75.35. The chrome exhaust tips and trailer hitch on this 1965 El Camino are owner-installed items.*

imposed on A-bodies as part of its anti-performance stance. Early 1964 reports mentioned much corporate infighting concerning the GTO and the displacement limit, and at one time the thinking was that the big-block Pontiac intermediate would be squelched after all.

"Many observers look for a knock-down, drag-out battle within top management over the performance policy in the next few months," claimed the July 1964 issue of *Motor Trend*. Meanwhile, Pontiac's Pete Estes boldly promoted the GTO contrary to his superior's best wishes, and Bunkie Knudsen's crew silently waited for its chance to unleash a true tiger-killer—not just a Corvette-powered small-block Chevelle, but a full-fledged, big-block brute.

Serious Chevelle performance roots date back to April 1963, when the ever-present Vince Piggins, Chevrolet Engineering's Product Performance chief, proposed a NASCAR-inspired Chevelle powered by the same "Mystery Motor" big-block V-8 that had scorched Daytona's super-speedway in February. Piggins' plan involved a run of one hundred Mark-

*A limited-edition promotional piece from the beginning, the 1965 Z16 Chevelle kicked off the SS 396 legacy in proud fashion. Available only as a fully loaded posh performer, the Z16 was steeply priced at roughly $4,200. Only 201 were built, including one mysterious convertible apparently used as a company fleet car before it disappeared into obscurity. Excluding that one convertible, which was painted Sierra Tan, exterior finishes for the remaining 200 Z16s numbered three: Regal Red; Tuxedo Black; or Crocus Yellow. The Z16's blacked-out grille would become an SS 396 tradition. Z16 Chevelle identification included the addition of the famed "396 Turbo Jet" crossflags on the front fenders and the relocation of the "Malibu SS" badges from the rear quarters to just behind the front wheel openings. The Z16's standard, mag-style wheelcover would become optional (RPO N96) for SS 396 Chevelles from 1966 to 1968.*

motored 1964 Malibu sport coupes with an extended 116in wheelbase to meet NASCAR's minimum standard for Grand National competition.

Chevy management gave an initial OK, despite GM's anti-racing edict. They built one test vehicle, powered by a 396ci derivative of the Mk II big-block, and in late 1963 Knudsen asked Smokey Yunick to take a peek. Yunick felt the car was no good for racing, thanks to its nose-heavy stance—the engine sat too high and too far forward. After the big-block's relocation that winter, Yunick's gang took the car for a tryout at the Firestone Test Track in Fort Stockton, Texas. Driven by Chevrolet engineer Doug Roe, the Chevelle ran nearly 10mph faster than a 396-equipped, full-sized Chevy, but was wrecked before it could prove itself at the 1964 Daytona 500.

*Gold-stripe tires on 14x6 rims were among the long list of standard Z16 equipment, as were the "love 'em or hate 'em" mag-style wheel covers. To set the Z16 apart in back, standard Malibu taillight lenses were exchanged for the less ornate 300 series units, and the rear quarter welds around the taillights (normally hidden by bright trim) were covered by a body-colored moulding. Capping off the exclusive look was an eye-catching, blacked-out panel for the lower half of the rear cove area.*

That accident, combined with the fact that development efforts failed to meet an NHRA deadline specifying that new models aimed at 1964 drag race competition be ready for review by November 10, 1963, negated any chance Piggins had of releasing a street-worthy 396 Chevelle for 1964. Although the project's delay lasted a year, it was a blessing in disguise, as Engineering was allowed ample time to perfect the package before it reached the public.

Meanwhile, the rumor mill continued churning. Big news in the summer of 1964 was GM's reversal of its 330ci limit for A-bodies, thanks undoubtedly to growing GTO popularity. Big-block intermediates from Buick and Olds were already in the works, and all that remained was for Chevrolet to join the race.

Noting that the addition of larger displacements in smaller cars was the coming thing, *Motor Trend* pointed out the obvious, explaining that 327 Corvette engines would never do if the Chevelle was to compete in "the booming GTO market." What would replace the Corvette V-8s? The answer was equally obvious.

"Chevrolet may revive the Mk. II Daytona engine for passenger car and truck use," announced *Motor Trend* in its September 1964 issue. "This is the engine that shook the troops at Daytona in '63, developing about 550 hp from 427 inches, giving lap speeds up to 166 mph. It disappeared when GM dropped out of racing. But recent reports mention '65 Chevelle prototypes under test powered by this basic engine reduced to 396ci—with hydraulic cam, street carburetion, and exhaust heat on the manifold. Acceleration is said to exceed that of the '409' Super/Stock engine in the big Chevrolet. This engine is ideal for use in high-performance compacts, because it weighs about 50 pounds less than the '409'—around 600 pounds complete. Look for this 396-cubic-inch super-performance Chevelle next spring."

Two months later, reports said that GM intended to raise its A-body displacement limit to 400ci, enough to allow a 396 Chevelle entry into the muscle car fraternity. Also mentioned were sales crews' pressures on the Engineering department to exchange the obsolete, two-speed Powerglide automatic for a modern, three-speed unit. If a hot 396 Chevelle was going to become reality, a superior three-speed automatic transmission was definitely needed. Both joined Chevrolet ranks in mid-1965.

In February Bunkie Knudsen did the introductory honors again, this time at Chevrolet's Mesa, Arizona, proving grounds. Long-rumored, the 396ci Mk IV big-block was finally unveiled in three forms: a serious, solid-lifter 425hp version for the Corvette; a more socially acceptable 375hp variety for the Chevelle; and a domestic, yet far from docile, 325hp example for the equally new Caprice Custom Sedan four-door hardtop.

Aimed at luxury buyers who perhaps preferred a little punch with their cake, the 396 Caprice offered yet another new feature, the three-speed Turbo Hydra-matic automatic transmission. Initially, rumors had Chevrolet building its own "three-speed Powerglide," leaving GM's existing three-speed automatic to the B-O-P people. But in the end, Chevrolet went with basically the same "Super Turbine Drive" transmission Buick had introduced in 1964, renaming it the "Turbo Hydra-matic" and mating it to the 325hp 396 for use in full-sized Chevys. As for a Chevelle application, it would be another two years before the Turbo Hydra-matic would become a Super Sport option.

Between the Caprice's 325hp Mark IV and the Corvette's dominating 425hp big-block, Knudsen introduced the 375hp 396 as part of the legendary Z16 package for the Chevelle SS. Specially designed for maximum publicity impact, the big-block Chev-

*Bucket seats and console for automatic and four-speed cars—three-speeds again got column shifters—continued as standard Super Sport interior features in 1965, and the look was basically unchanged overall. Here, this 1965 SS convertible is equipped with RPO N34—the simulated wood-grained steering wheel—in place of the deluxe steering wheel used as standard SS fare in both 1964 and 1965.*

elle was hustled off into the hands of eager journalists and high-profile celebrities. Reportedly, about half the cars were first used as promotional pieces, with the other half going into private hands through various dealers across the country.

Identified as "Custom Caprice Equipment" as a tie-in to Chevy's new full-sized offering, RPO Z16 was as tough to obtain as it was desirable. Chevrolet executed only a limited production run of 200 Z16 hardtops plus one convertible, all easily identified by their exclusive trim treatment and

Producing 195 maximum horsepower at 4800rpm, the standard 283ci V-8 was by no means a potent powerplant; nor, armed with a two-barrel carburetor, 9.25:1 compression, and single exhaust, was it meant to be. For those who preferred their *Super Sports* to be more super, there were three optional 327s: the 250hp L30; the 300hp L74; and the 350hp L79. Although the optional 220hp L77 283 had apparently been replaced for 1965 by the L30 327, some reports claim it may have reappeared in February 1965.

wheelcovers. In back, much of the typical Chevelle rear cove brightwork was removed and a blacked-out panel featuring three parallel mouldings was added, as was a "Malibu SS 396" emblem near the right taillight. On the rear quarters, the familiar "Malibu SS" emblems were also deleted, leaving a clean, uncluttered appearance, while the front fenders got a little overcrowded with the relocated SS

identification and the soon-to-be legendary "396 Turbo Jet" crossflags.

The wheelcovers were distinctive, stamped-steel, mag-type designs that onlookers either loved or hated. *Motor Trend*'s John Ethridge felt they were "the most handsome and authentic-looking simulated custom wheels we've seen." On the other side of the coin, *Car Life*'s wheelcover critics called them "the homeliest phony 'mag-wheel' hubcaps imaginable."

Exclusive treatment carried over inside, where mandatory Z16 options included a padded instrument panel, a 6000rpm tach, a 160mph speedometer, a dash-mounted clock, deluxe front seat belts with retractors, rear seat belts, and Chevrolet's new AM/FM Mutiplex stereo radio. Hung beneath the dash, the Multiplex unit filled the car with sound through four speakers: two in the rear package shelf; one each in the front kick panels. "There's nothing in this world, Charlie," wrote

*Mechanix Illustrated*'s Tom McCahill, "like slipping down the turnpike being belted in the back by 375 horsepower and in the ear by 4-speaker Bach-power!"

It is believed that two 1965 Chevelles were originally taken off the Baltimore assembly line and delivered to Chevrolet Engineering in Warren, Michigan, to become Z16 "engineering studies," while all other Z16s were built at the Leeds plant in Kansas

*At the top of the small-block heap in 1965 was this 327 V-8, RPO L79. With free-breathing heads, a Holley four-barrel, and some serious 11:1 compression, the L79 pumped out 350hp at 5800rpm, and 360lb-ft of torque at 3600rpm. The air cleaner decal is incorrect; other than the Z16's 396 big-block, none of the Super Sport V-8s in 1964 and 1965 carried engine identification on their air cleaners. This L79 is also equipped with an incorrect Corvette intake manifold.*

Like its stillborn L76 forerunner, the bold L79 small-block featured full engine dress-up—bright valve covers and dual-snorkel air cleaner—and announced its presence through these decals. In all, 6,021 of these hot little V-8s found their way into Chevelles and El Caminos in 1965.

City, Missouri. Once off the line, many went to VIPs, celebrities, and members of the automotive press, or became company fleet cars, all part of a plan to obtain as much exposure as possible.

Chevrolet presented Z16s to high-profile men like Briggs Cunningham, Phil Hill, A. J. Foyt, and Dan Blocker, "people who would be likely to drive them as transportation to Riverside, Watkins Glen, Indy, Daytona, Elkhart, country clubs and the like," according to a Chevrolet memo. Clearly the biggest of these big men, Blocker played "Hoss" on "Bonanza," the popular television western sponsored

*Standard Z16 interior features included seat belts front and rear, AM/FM four-speaker stereo, dash-mounted clock, 160mph speedometer, 6000rpm tachometer, and an oil gauge. Options appearing here include power windows and the RPO N34 simulated wood-grained sport steering wheel. Interior color choices included black, white, and red, with the latter not being available if Crocus Yellow was chosen as the exterior finish. Redlining at 5700rpm, the 1965 Malibu SS 396's 6000rpm tach, RPO U16, was one of many "mandatory options" included when customers requested the $1,501.05 Z16 package.*

by Chevrolet. It was this connection that probably explains Technical Projects Manager W. R. MacKenzie's futile suggestion that the 396 Chevelle be named "Maverick," a moniker later snatched up by Ford for an entirely different animal.

Though shot down in the name game, MacKenzie continued to push promotionally, proposing in a memo dated March 3, 1965, that the rest of the "Bonanza" cast be allowed behind the wheel of a Z16, "no doubt to keep peace in the family, as well as to spread publicity value." No ifs, ands, or buts about it, publicity was the Z16's most prominent purpose.

That's not to say the Z16 was only a tease. Imagery and pizzazz were part of the package, sure, but so too was a heavy dose of serious performance. Engineers started by building Chevy's first 396 Chevelle on a convertible boxed frame to guarantee rigid surefootedness. Along with being stronger throughout, the frame incorporated two additional body mounts.

The suspension, too, was beefed. Stiffer coils and shocks at all four corners both checked body roll and attempted to make up for the 690lb of Mk IV big-block under the hood. A large, 1.06in sway bar in front, and an-

other torsional stabilizer tying the boxed lower control arms together in back, also limited roll, as did the two supports mounted between pivot points of the upper and lower control arms. The rigid frame, stiff springs, and reinforced four-link suspension

*Chevrolet general manager Semon E. "Bunkie" Knudsen poses proudly with the Z16 Chevelle he introduced at Chevrolet's Mesa, Arizona, proving grounds in February 1965.*

*Below*
*Engine dress-up typically was included with the L37 396 big-block V-8, the heart of RPO Z16. Chrome valve covers, a die-cast "396" crossflag emblem, and a chrome lid for the dual-snorkel air cleaner helped in the image department, while 375hp and 420lb-ft of torque backed up that image with real muscle.*

# Chapter 4

# 1966–1967

## *Big-Block or No Block*

"One of the pluses of the SS 396 option is an improved suspension. The SS 396s were the first GM intermediates we've driven that were free of the rear-end jello-roll blues that make life so hard for back-seat passengers, and give the driver a few 'moments' as well. The SS 396 is far and away the best handling and riding GM product we've driven in a long time."
—Robert Schilling, *Motor Trend*

As a high-profile promotional piece, Chevrolet's sizzling Z16 Chevelle had done its job well in 1965, warming the hearts of countless street performance fans, many who'd almost given up on the Bow-Tie guys. By 1966, big-block intermediates—already known as "muscle cars"—represented the only way to fly, and Chevelle customers would finally get their tickets. Super Sport Chevelles, cars that had appeared in basic form powered by frugal six-cylinders in 1964 and 1965, became truly super in 1966. Gone were sixes and small-blocks; in their place was one powerplant only, the muscular 396ci Mk IV V-8.

A true eye-catcher on the street, the 1966 SS 396 was based on a nicely restyled, sleek, Malibu hardtop body that remained exceptionally clean but replaced the previous boxy A-body lines with a mildly stated "Coke bot-

*Opposite*
*Offering ample performance at a far more affordable price than its Z16 forerunner, Chevrolet's Super Sport Chevelle came only one way for 1966—with 396 Turbo Jet power up front. No more small-blocks; just three different levels of Mk IV big-block brute force.*

*Along with the rear quarter script, 1966 Super Sports got "SS 396" badges on the right side of the rear cove panel, which was painted body color on nearly all 1966 SS 396s. Initially, brochures showed a blacked-out treatment for the tail*

*(reminiscent of the 1965 Z16), and apparently some cars did receive this feature. How many, however, is not known. The blacked-out rear panel would become an SS 396 feature in 1967, and remain so until 1971.*

*Unlike in 1964 and 1965, the standard 1966 Super Sport interior featured a bench seat—buckets and a console were optional. Options in this case include the simulated wood-grained steering wheel, the infamous* "knee-knocker" *tach, and the Multiplex four-speaker stereo. That long shifter is attached to an ultra-rare M22* "Rock Crusher" *four-speed—only twelve M22s were ordered in 1966.*

tle" form and a sporty, recessed rear window. Appropriate "SS 396" emblems in the blacked-out grille and on the rear cove panel, "Super Sport" rear quarter script, and those legendary "396 Turbo Jet" front fender crossflags added to the attraction. So, too, did a pair of aggressive-looking hood bulges trimmed with nonfunctional grilles.

Although brochures initially showed a blacked-out rear cove panel, few 1966 SS 396s apparently came with that treatment. Color-accented rocker and lower rear quarter mouldings; wheel opening trim; 7.75x14 redline tires on wide, 6in rims; and small

*The Z16's blacked-out grille, "396 Turbo Jet" crossflags, and simulated mag-style wheelcovers carried over into 1966 as Super Sport features, although the wheelcovers were optional—standard items were simple "dog-dish" center caps on 14x6 JK rims. "SS 396" identification in the grille, the attractive "twin-bulge" hood, and "Super Sport" rear quarter script made up the list of new 1966 SS exterior items. Wheel opening trim and lower body sill mouldings were also standard Super Sport fare.*

"dog-dish" hubcaps completed the standard SS 396 exterior package, which, like its small-block and six-cylinder predecessors, was also available in convertible form.

Save for the doggie-style wheelcovers, basic SS 396 imagery represented a decent response to earlier requests for a more suitable big-block Chevelle fashion statement. In its September 1965 review of the Z16 Malibu, *Car Life* claimed that "the fellow who puts out the kind of money this equipment costs wants something that shows it; what's the use of buying it if no one can tell it from the neighbors' Powerglide Slick-Six?"

According to *Hot Rod*'s Eric Dahlquist, the neighbors never had a chance once you rolled a 1966 SS 396 into your driveway. "Any way you look at it there's something special about the Chevelle," he wrote. "Take the keen outline of the pseudo-fastback roof, or the hood ventilators, or everything—it's great." And if you didn't like the dog-dish caps, those "love 'em or hate 'em" simulated magwheels made famous/infamous on the Z16 were a few extra dollars away on the

49

*"Strato-buckets," RPO A52, represented the optional choice for the buyer who wanted a truly sporty Super Sport interior in 1966. Headrests, RPO A81, were also optional, as was the floor console with clock, found under RPO number D55.*

options list under RPO N96. Also available was another simulated dress-up item, the P02 wire wheelcover, a style even less popular than the fake mags—10,814 buyers chose the N96 option in 1966, but only 6,974 checked off RPO P02.

Not everyone was won over as easily as Dahlquist, however. Comparing apples to oranges always represents a losing proposition, and so it was when it came time to make a stand concerning Chevrolet's 1966 SS 396. Spoiled by what they saw in 1965, some among the automotive press couldn't warm up completely to what represented a watered-down, regular-production rendition of the high-priced, high-powered Z16 ideal.

"Chevrolet tantalized us with the '65 version," claimed *Motorcade*'s John Lawlor, "leading us to believe that it had a superior entry in the supercar field. It did—last year. For '66, the Chevelle 396 has become a more routine, more conventional automobile." At least Lawlor remained fair, pointing out that the 1965 Z16 was "an expensive limited-edition that cost more than $4100. The new one is designed to be a bestseller and has a price book that opens at only $2776."

Chevrolet's first 396 Chevelle was an exclusive preview built as one specific package with one specific purpose—promoting future big-block Chevelle production. Affordability, customer preference, and mass market appeal weren't factors. "So you didn't want the stereo?" asked Lawlor. "Sorry, but you couldn't get the big engine without it." But the 1966 SS 396 was a different breed, a reasonably affordable performance car to be built "in immense quantities... with—and without—all sorts of optional equip-

ment." Quipped Lawlor, "no longer did you *have* to take that stereo!"

Chevrolet's marketing experts *did* take mass market appeal into account once it came time to transform the tantalizing Z16 into the more saleable SS 396. The watering down (if you will) of the original 396 Chevelle package was only smart, given that the fully optioned 1965 Z16 remained out of reach of the average performance customer. "One can only guess that the original 396 [Chevelle] just didn't fill the bill as a machine a great number of people would like to be married to for 36 payments," wrote Dahlquist. "After all, image or no, this is why the thing is on the market."

Tom McCahill's "four-speaker Bach-power" wasn't the only item left behind as part of Chevrolet's repackaging of the basic 396 Chevelle. Cost cutting also did away with the rigid convertible boxed frame, the exceptional 11in drum brakes, and the rear stabilizer bar. Features like the Z16's tach and the earlier Super Sport's bucket seats became added-cost options. Topping it off, the serious 375hp L37 was replaced as the standard SS 396 powerplant by the much milder 325hp big-block, an engine also available at extra cost under 1966 El Camino hoods as RPO L35.

Perhaps proving that cost cutting wasn't everyone's goal, nearly a third of SS 396 buyers passed up the standard 325hp 396 in 1966, opting instead for RPO L34, the 360hp 396. Both engines relied on 10.25:1 compression, while the hotter L34 used a lumpier cam and an optional 585cfm Holley four-barrel carb, and was based on the beefier four-bolt main block.

*Motorcade*'s Lawlor tested an L34 1966 SS 396 and came away predictably disappointed—"predictably" because of his obvious preference for the hot-blooded Z16. Accordingly, he felt the new SS 396 was "much looser, partly because of the lighter, more flexible frame." With a smaller,

15/16in front sway bar, body roll was more pronounced as well. On the other hand, revised spring rates front and rear helped minimize the nose-heavy plowing in turns inherent to most big-block intermediates, a negative feature that all who drove the Z16 noticed in a hurry. Nonetheless, Lawlor naturally felt the first 396 Chevelle handled better. "Any feeling of nose-heaviness it may have had was much less discomforting than the new car's swaying."

Although the standard SS 396 chassis wasn't as stout as the Z16's, springs were still thirty percent stiffer than stock Chevelle units. Also included was the hefty 12-bolt rear end, with its 8.875in ring gear, and the invaluable rear suspension frame supports located between the upper and lower control arm mounting points. Used in 1965 on the Z16, as well as with the optional L74 and L79 small-blocks, the frame supports remained a standard

SS 396 feature in 1966. The 12-bolt rear, another carryover, housed 3.31:1 gears behind the 325hp 396 with manual transmission; specifying the L34 upped the axle ratio ante to 3.73:1. Optional ratios went as low as 4.88:1.

Lawlor found the standard SS 396 brakes to be of major concern, and rightly so. Like so many American muscle cars of the sixties, stopping reaction took a backseat to its opposite action. Exchanging the Impala's 11in drums for the standard Chevelle units was "an inexcusable regression. Any car with this one's potential perfor-

*In base form, the 396 Turbo Jet for the 1966 Chevelle SS rated at 325hp. Optional power came in the form of the 360hp L34 big-block and the somewhat mysterious 375hp L78, of which 3,099 were installed beneath Chevelle and Custom El Camino hoods. New for 1966, the open-element air cleaner would become an SS 396 standard.*

*Although an average performer, the standard 325hp SS 396 could still throw its weight around. Based on a two-bolt main bearing block, the 325hp Mk IV big-block, labeled RPO L35 for El Camino applications, produced maximum power at 4800rpm; maximum torque of 410ft-lbs came at 3200rpm.*

mance should have the biggest, strongest brakes possible," Lawlor wrote.

He wasn't alone in making this conclusion. "While the 9.5x2.5 molded asbestos binders are at least equal to the task of everyday traffic," reported *Hot Rod*'s Dahlquist, "successive stops

from over 60 are not their forte." Help was available, however, in the form of RPO J65, sintered-metallic brake linings which, according to Dahlquist, stopped "on a dime over and over again without temperamental displays."

Dahlquist and Lawlor also agreed on transmission choices. A heavy-duty three-speed was standard equipment, with three four-speeds and the aging Powerglide automatic waiting on the options list. Granted, a four-speed was the real man's choice—with the exceptionally rare M22 "Rock Crusher" being the ultimate macho preference—but if rowing your own wasn't your idea of performance driving, the two-

speed Powerglide was a poor alternative.

"Probably most interesting of all Chevy transmissions," Dahlquist wrote, "is the one which isn't even being offered in the Chevelle line—the three-speed Turbo Hydra-matic." Mated in full-sized applications to the 427 Mk IV big-block, the Turbo Hydra-matic had yet to trickle down to the 396 A-bodies, much to the dismay of Lawlor, who claimed the Powerglide was "too outdated and inefficient to be of much interest to the kind of buyer who'd want a Chevelle 396. Why [the Turbo Hydra-matic] isn't available in the SS 396 is a mystery. The tired, old Chevy two-speed unit just isn't in the same league as the crisp, efficient three-speed automatics obtainable in the Chevelle's competitors from Ford, Mercury, Dodge and Plymouth." Keeping up with the Joneses would have to wait until 1967.

Overall, the *Motorcade* writer concluded, the 1966 SS 396 was a "good road car," but corporate compromising had "taken away its edge." As he put it, "we missed the thundering performance and the taut chassis feel we'd experienced in last year's model. In fact, you know something? We even missed the stereo!"

Lawlor had a right to his opinion, of course—when compared to the Z16, the basic 1966 SS 396 *did* pale. Even with the optional 360hp 396, the best performance *Motorcade*'s testers could extract was a 15.5 second/91mph quarter-mile. But, as mentioned, pitting the limited-edition Z16 against the regular-production SS 396 was simply not a fair test. Lawlor was the first to admit that fact, pointing out that the 1966 SS 396 had less compression, less cam, smaller ports and valves, and something else the 1965 car didn't have to lug around: an air pump.

The pump, mandatory on all SS 396s sold in California beginning in 1966, was RPO K19, part of Chevrolet's "Air Injection Reactor" emissions controls. Requiring a special carburetor and distributor, the AIR system injected oxygen into the exhaust flow, reducing pollutant counts while also restricting performance. According to Lawlor, the system stifled "breathing ability, especially at top end...[making] it all but impossible to grab that last, crucial 1000 to 1500 rpm needed for the quickest acceleration." Luckily for performance buyers, RPO K19 wasn't required in the other forty-nine states, although by 1968 it would become standard SS 396 equipment in manual transmission applications.

The efforts of *Popular Hot Rodding*'s George Elliott, who tested a 1966 SS 396 nearly identical to the one flogged by *Motorcade,* were of special interest to California car owners. After scoring similar numbers at the track, Elliott disconnected the smog pump and applied some "proper strip tuning," resulting in a startling 14.4-second run down the quarter that terminated at 100mph. Potential was

*Demonstrating the standard SS 396 dog-dish wheel covers, this 1966 Super Sport convertible was one of 5,429 built.*

clearly there, even if face value wasn't.

That potential became even greater soon after Lawlor let his feelings be known. An announcement in *Motor Trend*'s June issue detailed yet another optional big-block for the SS 396. According to the report, the new L78 396 was "about equivalent to last year's Z16 except for a solid lifter cam and new exhaust manifolds to more conveniently fit the Chevelle chassis. It's rated the same 375 bhp at 5600 rpm and it uses the big-valve heads of the 427, 11:1 compression and a big-port aluminum intake manifold with big [780cfm] Holley four-barrel." Big news indeed. Concluded *Motor Trend,* "the engine should put the Chevelle SS right up front in the supercar market."

Unlike Lawlor, many felt the 1966 SS 396 was "right up front" long before the L78 came along. Even though *Hot Rod*'s Dahlquist managed only a 15.70/92 best in the quarter behind the wheel of a 360hp SS 396, he recognized both the car's true potential and the fact that performance cars had to serve as everyday transportation for most people. Price, roadability, comfort, and such, were every bit as important as muscle flexing. Dahlquist

*It was advertising tactics like these that would have GM's front office scrambling to clean up its image a mere one year down the road. With safety crusaders in Washington growing less tolerant of the apparent disregard for highway safety displayed by the mere presence of Detroit's muscle cars, to depict a car as wild and ferocious was considered "too suggestive."*

*Drag racer Wally Booth helped his sponsors gain loads of publicity by taking SS/D honors with his 1966 SS 396 at the NHRA Winternationals in 1967, setting a world record along the way. Engle Cams also used Booth's record-setting achievement to sell their performance hardware (which, by the way, Booth had used to help set his record).*

concluded that the SS 396 had "just the right measures of ride-handling and acceleration that would make it the nuts for all kinds of driving, especially long trips. It's a fun car for today's dull traffic, and if it helps relieve the tedium of travel, you can't ask much more."

Earlier, *Car and Driver* had given the 1966 SS 396 similar marks after an intriguing six-car showdown that pitted the Chevelle against "America's fastest sport sedans"—Oldsmobile's 442, Pontiac's GTO, Buick's Gran Sport, Ford's Fairlane GTA, and Mercury's Cyclone GT (Dodge and Plymouth diplomatically declined invitations to the meet). Although the SS 396 finished next to last in acceleration trials (14.66 seconds at 99.88mph), *Car and Driver*'s staff rated it right behind the champion Olds in an overall scoring system that took forty variables into account.

Read *Car and Driver*'s bottom line: "The SS 396 is not the fastest car or the best handling, but it is possibly the best compromise of them all, especially when its relatively low price is considered. It is a new car on the market and you can rest assured its development has just begun. On that basis, we think the Chevelle deserves second spot by a wide margin."

Maybe that's why SS 396 sales nearly matched those of the 1965 small-block Super Sports, cars that supposedly possessed a wider market appeal. Then again, market demands do change, especially when the competition injects new variables into the formula, as Pontiac had done in 1964. Two years later, the popularity of Detroit's big-block intermediates—all the newborn muscle machines *Car and Driver* had so faithfully attempted to compare—was just gathering steam. How far automakers would go in this rapidly escalating horsepower war was anyone's guess.

SS 396 sales reached 72,272 for 1966, representing a hefty seventeen percent of total Chevelle production. Chevrolet officials, surely hoping much of that success would carry over into 1967, ended up a tad disappointed. Obligated to one more year in the A-body styling cycle at a time when increasing competition seemingly turned brand new into old news in a heart-

beat, the Super Sport design crew did its best to remake the popular 1966 image for an encore appearance.

Body lines remained unchanged, with the most noticeable tweaks typically coming at the nose and tail. For 1966, the blacked-out SS 396 grille had wrapped around the front corners, while recessed taillights remained within their boundaries. For 1967, a slightly restyled blackened grille came to an end at each fender point, while less distinctive taillights became wraparound units in back. Assisting in the distinctive department was a new SS 396 rear cove panel, also done in black. Two redesigned, simulated hood "scoops" and reshuffled "Super Sport" script on the rear quarters helped set off the 1967 SS 396, as did two differ-

ent types of optional lower bodyside stripes.

Underneath, the basic SS 396 engineering package rolled on essentially unchanged, with the exception of an advertised decrease in optional power. The 325hp 396 was still standard, but the street racer's choice, the L34 High Performance big-block, dropped 10hp down to 350, probably more as a public relations ploy than as a relative measure of output.

By 1967, those ever-present sticks-in-the-mud up on the fourteenth floor were again at work putting the squelch on speed, a predictable move when you noted that GM's so-called anti-performance corporate stance had gone bowlegged since its infamous anti-racing edict had been passed

*Although Chevrolet was supposedly "out of racing," that didn't stop the legendary Smokey Yunick from building a 1966 Chevelle for NASCAR competition. Created with a little help through Chevrolet Engineering's "back door," his #13 Chevelle appeared at the 1967 Daytona 500 and promptly won the pole. Called a "beautifully handcrafted 15/16-scale model of the genuine article" by* Hot Rod's *Eric Dahlquist, Yunick's Chevelle had the competition and NASCAR officials up in arms—and for good reason. That the tech inspector's stock body form template wouldn't fit Yunick's downsized sheet metal was just the tip of the rule-bending iceberg. Yunick's return to the Daytona 500 in 1968 with an even more radical 1966 Chevelle only brought about a more dedicated attempt to thwart his efforts—his second #13 Chevelle was banned from Daytona and never raced a lap.*

The easiest way to identify a 1967 SS 396 from the rear is by the distinctive, blacked-out rear cove panel. New taillights and the stacked "Super Sport" rear quarter script are additional clues. As in 1966, 7.75x14 red line tires on 14x6 JK rims with dog dish center caps were standard for the SS 396, but new for 1967 were F70 Wide Ovals when the optional L34 and L78 engines were ordered.

down in January 1963. First the GTO had slipped through, followed shortly by Oldsmobile's 442 and Buick's Gran Sport. A tough sell on the idea of big-block intermediates from the start, GM's front office subtly began pulling back the reigns not long after the regular-production SS 396 hit the streets for 1966.

In the spring of 1966, "a usually reliable authority" informed journalist Roger Huntington of GM's intentions to "back off even more on high-performance cars in 1967." Per Huntington's report in *Motor Trend's* July 1966 issue, the plan involved doing away with multiple carburetor options and clamping down on over-aggressive advertising, pitches that might incite the natives too zealously. Also mentioned was an "edict that no production-line models can be marketed with a weight/bhp ratio under 10 lb. per bhp." In intermediate ranks, this limit roughly translated into—you guessed it—350 horsepower.

According to Huntington, ever-growing attention to automobile safety was one of the motivating factors behind GM's stepped-up efforts to tone down its muscular image. The revamped 1967 Chevelle incorporated a host of new standard safety features as it was, all added in an attempt to

appease the congressional gods of fear-free highway travel. But apparently there was more to the move than that.

"GM brass sees a way to put Ford and Chrysler on the hot seat, and get out of the bad-guy limelight," wrote Huntington. "GM for years has been the focal point for the major portion of anti-automobile attention in this country. Now, with all this anti-performance safety talk, and with Ford and Chrysler deeply involved in million-dollar racing programs, GM sees a way out." Customers, however, didn't see things quite the same. As Huntington put it, "performance fans will read it and weep!"

Initial repercussions weren't as serious as Huntington made out, although his report explains why the hot 375hp L78 SS 396 seemingly went un-

Other than revised rocker trim and a new grille and bumper, practically everything about the 1967 SS 396 was a direct carry-over from 1966, right down to the standard dog-dish wheelcovers, which perhaps helps to explain why sales went down for the year. For 1967, the familiar "SS 396" badge returned to the center of the grille, which became less blacked-out thanks to the addition of parallel bright bars running side to side.

*SS 396 Chevelles finally got an "SS" steering wheel in 1967—no identification had appeared on early Super Sport wheels. Also, notice the new location for the optional tach—better than the "knee-knocker" of 1966, but still difficult to read while rowing through the gears. Relocating the 7000rpm tach to the upper left corner of the dash served only to totally obscure the left-hand turn signal indicator and partially block the view of the fuel gauge. Designers added the hidden indicator to the tach's face; viewing the gas gauge simply required a little extra effort.*

derground in 1967. Listed separately on a Chevrolet internal specifications sheet in 1966, the impressive L78 was nowhere to be found in official 1967 promotional literature, labelled instead as a "dealer-installed" option. Anyone wanting to flaunt mid-sized Bow-Tie might in the faces of GM front office killjoys needed to fork over an additional $475.80 on top of the 350hp L34's $105.35 asking price. That figure, along with the lack of publicity, leaves little wonder why

only 612 L78s were sold in 1967, compared to the reported 3,099 375hp 396s snapped up the previous year.

Less intimidating from a price perspective were two new options that helped enhance SS 396 performance as well as overall appeal. RPO J52, priced at $79, added power front disc brakes, while checking off M40 on the options list mated the long-awaited Turbo Hydra-matic three-speed automatic to the 396. For 1967, the $147.45 Turbo Hydra-matic transmis-

sion was made available in A-body applications for only the SS 396 and the 396-equipped El Camino, much to the pleasure of performance buyers who preferred shiftless driving.

For performance buyers who preferred not making contact with immovable objects, RPO J52 was just the ticket, featuring big, 11in discs, and Bendix four-piston calipers. Fade resistance probably represented the discs' main attraction as *Motor Trend*'s Robert Schilling reported a slight edge in stopping distances from 60mph for a drum brake SS 396, an edge he predicted would undoubtedly disappear once the drums heated up. "We still regard disc brakes as a bargain option," he concluded. A set of sporty Rally wheels featuring bright trim rings and center caps made the J52 deal even more attractive. Specially vented for the disc brake application through slots in the rim center, the soon-to-be-popular Rally wheels measured the same as the stock 14x6 units.

As for the entire 1967 package, Schilling, after a test session with a 325hp SS 396, a 375hp L78, and a 325hp 396 El Camino, came away duly impressed. Quarter-mile acceleration figures—at 15.9/89, 14.9/96.5, and 15.7/90, respectively—were predictable, but the *Motor Trend* reviewer was attracted by more than speed.

"One of the pluses that goes with the SS 396 option is an improved suspension," he wrote. "The SS 396s were the first GM intermediates we've driven that were free of the rear-end jello-roll blues that make life so hard for backseat passengers, and give the driver a few 'moments' as well. This phenomenon [is] caused by coil springs, inadequate rear axle locations, and poor shock absorbers. The SS 396 breaks away from this negative image and is far and away the best handling and riding GM product we've driven in a long time."

Naturally, Schilling did have a complaint or two, the most prominent concerning the inside of the 1967 SS 396. One involved the four-speed shifter's nasty habit of jamming the driver's thumb against the seat while going for second, the other, typically, concerned tach location. As in 1966, the standard 1967 SS 396 interior fea-

Although basically identical, the SS 396 power lineup for 1967 featured one adjustment. Standard still was the 325hp big-block, shown here, followed by the L34 revised down to 350hp. At the top remained the rare 375hp L78, of which only 602 were sold in 1967.

59

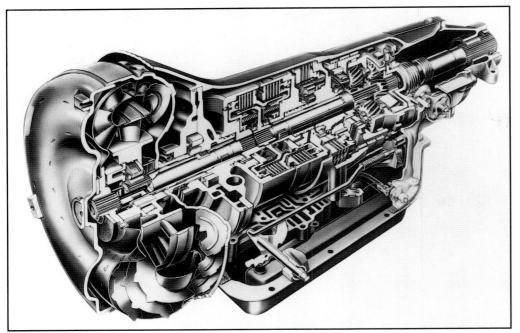

*Chevrolet's durable three-speed Turbo Hydra-matic automatic transmission finally made its appearance as an SS 396 option in 1967, two years after it first appeared in full-size ranks behind the Mk IV big-blocks. Shown here is a cutaway of the 1966 version.*

tured a bench seat, with Strato-buckets, console, and tachometer included at extra cost. Poorly located below the dash and to the right of the steering column in 1966, the appropriately tagged "knee-knocker" tach was moved to the dashboard's upper left-hand corner for 1967, a location Schilling felt was an improvement, "but Chevrolet had better keep looking."

"With hands in the quarter-to-three position," he explained, "our left fist was in the way." More important, the optional tach was mounted in front of the gas gauge, making a peek at the fuel level a "deliberate project." Also obscuring the left turn signal indicator, the tach did include a replacement indicator on its face, "showing that someone at Chevy is thinking."

Instrumental antics aside, the SS 396 was *Motor Trend's* choice for performance buyers who "dig power along with posh." Sales, however, dipped to 63,006 for 1967, thanks in part to the big-block Chevelle's "carryover" status working in concert with some fierce competition in the burgeoning muscle car market. Still, 60,000-plus production was nothing to sneeze at, nor was SS 396 popularity. With the exception of its corporate cousin at Pontiac, no other big-block intermediate turned as many heads in 1967 as Chevrolet's Super Sport Chevelle.

*Along with the Turbo Hydra-matic transmission, another well-received new option for the 1967 SS 396 were front disc brakes. Front discs, RPO J52, came with a set of attractive 14x6 Rally wheels specially vented to help cool the brakes.*

Although Chevrolet didn't build an SS 396 El Camino by name until 1968, everything but the moniker was available in both 1966 and 1967. This 1967 Custom El Camino features both the optional mag-style wheelcovers and the 396 Turbo Jet V-8, as demonstrated by the familiar crossflags on the front fenders.

Below
Bruce Larson's "USA-1" 1967 Chevelle was a popular ground-pounder on the match race circuit in the late sixties. A 427 stroked up to 454ci powered Larson's patriotic Super Sport to eight-second quarter-mile passes at more than 170mph.

# Chapter 5

# 1968–1969

## *The Long and Short of It*

"Although it is not the fastest machine right off the showroom floor, it does possess much more potential than any other car in its field. With a minimum cash outlay and a lot of elbow grease, this car can be [a] street eliminator any night of the week. Chevy may not be in racing, but its cars sure are!"

—Lee Kelley, *Popular Hot Rodding*

Long hood, short deck—it was a combo perhaps made most famous in April 1964 with the introduction of Ford's wildly popular Mustang, although Dearborn's little pony car was by no means the first to show off the look. Studebaker had long toyed with essence of the image, and the fiberglass-bodied Avanti probably wore it as well as anything on wheels. Nevertheless, it was the pony car breed that is best remembered for putting the long hood/short deck theme to use, beginning in 1964 with the Mustang and Plymouth's less-renowned Barracuda, followed three years later by Mercury's Cougar, Chevy's Camaro, and Pontiac's Firebird.

*Opposite*
*An overdue facelift gave the attractive 1968 Malibu body a pronounced long hood / short rear deck combination comparable to pony cars like the Camaro and Ford's Mustang. A one-inch wider tread also made for a more aggressive stance. Products of escalating safety concerns, the new side marker lamps up front also incorporated the nearly unnoticeable "396" identification. At a glance from a profile view, the 1968 SS 396 could have easily passed for a standard Malibu.*

*One item that helped set a 1968 SS 396 apart from the run-of-the-mill Chevelle crowd was its exclusive lower body treatment. All but dark-colored Super Sports got a blacked-out section below the lower bodyside trim. Adding the optional pinstripes, RPO D96, deleted that treatment, although early models apparently came with both.*

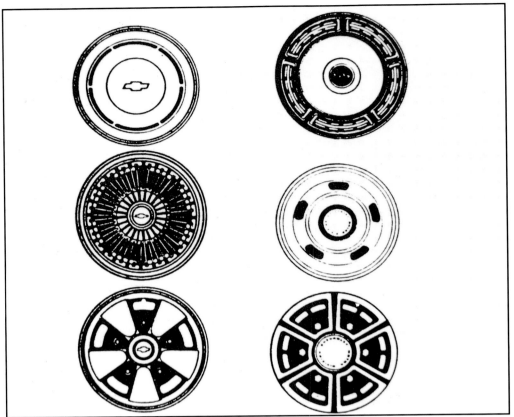

*Standard Super Sport wheelcovers for 1968 were the small center caps at upper left. Priced at $21.10, Full-sized Malibu wheelcovers with an "SS" insert (upper right) were available under RPO P01, as were the carryover simulated wire wheelcovers (middle at left), RPO N95, which cost $73.75. For the same price, an SS 396 buyer could also chose between the*

*N96 mag-style wheelcover (lower left) or the new PA2 "mag-spoke" design (lower right). Only 999 Chevelle customers chose the latter in 1968. Available for all 1968 SS 396s, regardless of the type of front brakes installed, was the 14x6 Rally wheel, RPO ZJ7, with a slightly restyled center cap (middle right). ZJ7 wheels were priced at $31.60.*

By 1968, the look had made its way up GM's pecking order into the intermediate ranks, appearing less pronounced than in pony car form but clearly present and accounted for. Somewhat of an optical illusion, the long hood/short deck image came about as part of a fresh remake of the A-body platform, a package that had remained untouched beneath the skin since its introduction late in 1963. Helping fool the eyes of Chevelle beholders were various new styling and design features, not the least of which was a revamped chassis.

Still based on the same type of perimeter frame, albeit a beefier design, the 1968 Chevelle chassis came in two wheelbases: one for two-door models; another for four-doors, wag-

ons, and El Caminos. Before 1968, all Chevelles, regardless of how many doors they had, measured 115in from hub to hub; for 1968, two-doors rode on a 112in wheelbase, while the rest got a longer, 116in chassis.

Although they lost 3in between the wheels, two-door Chevelles remained essentially identical to their 1967 counterparts in overall length, at 197in. The arrangement resulted in some serious overhang up front, making the lengthened 1968 hood appear even longer. Meanwhile, the trade of the 1967 Chevelle's recessed rear window for flush-mounted rear glass in a quasi-fastback design enhanced the shortened nature of the rear deck. The resulting impression was pure pony car, even though the new Chev-

elle was certainly a horse of another color.

Chevelle sheet metal for 1968 took its cue from "GM's 'coke bottle' school of styling," as *Motor Trend* called it, a form first applied ever so lightly to the 1966 A-body. Embodied fully in 1968 by the redesigned Corvette, "Coke bottle" imagery featured bulging rear quarters leading into a narrowed midsection, a look that suited the Chevelle's long-hood/short-deck layout to a T. Rounded bodysides with a lowered beltline, the sweeping roofline, a windshield raked back an additional 1.5in, and a forward-slanted nose all contributed to an aggressive impression not lost on curbside kibitzers. *Super Stock*'s Jim McCraw minced few words, calling the 1968 Chevelle a "smashingly beautiful car." Although *Car Life*'s critics felt the front overhang was impractical and excessive, they concluded that overall looks were sleek, "and must be considered contemporary."

Contributing to the sleek, contemporary look in SS 396 garb were hideaway windshield wipers, standard equipment for the new, luxury-minded Concours Chevelle and all Malibu models. Additional SS 396 exterior equipment carried on in much the same fashion, with two exceptions. Remaining in place were "SS 396" emblems front and rear, twin hood bulges, and the black-accented grille and rear cove panel. Gone, however, was the "Super Sport" rear quarter script, and engine identification was relegated to an almost unnoticeable tag incorporated into the side marker lamp bezels up front, new items for 1968 inspired by ever-tightening federal safety standards.

Stylists added a contrasting black lower body treatment for 1968 SS 396s, perhaps as a trade-off for the loss of the revered Turbo Jet cross-flags. Representing the easiest way to quickly identify a big-block Chevelle from a profile perspective in 1968, the black lower section wasn't used on dark-colored Super Sports. This treatment was also deleted when the eye-catching RPO D96 pinstripes (available in black, white, or red) were added, although 1968 SS 396s built before December 1, 1967, apparently carried both the D96 stripes and the black-painted section. Stripes and lower body adornment aside, the 1968 SS 396 could turn heads with ease. "It'd be a big mover on looks alone," beamed Chevrolet ads.

Of course, the beauty of this beast went more than skin deep. As in 1966 and 1967, the domesticated 325hp 396 supplied standard power, with the 350hp L34 available for another $105.35. Still somewhat of a secret, at least at the beginning of the model year, the truly hot 375hp L78 396 finally made an appearance on order sheets in 1968—if only on the back—and 4,751 buyers checked it off with a vengeance. Transmission choices carried over as well; standard equipment was a three-speed manual followed by the M20 wide-ratio four-speed, the M21 close-ratio four-speed (for the L34 and L78 only), and the no-nonsense M22 Rock Crusher (available behind the L78). Both the M35 Powerglide and M40 three-speed Turbo Hydra-matic automatics were listed as well.

Once they hit the streets, the new Super Sport Chevelles inspired responses that ranged from raves to rejections, though it was clear the SS 396 image ranked at the top of the muscle car heap as far as the average buyer was concerned. "Since the beginning, the SS 396 Chevelle has been thought of by GM fans as inferior to only the GTO as a street-strip intermediate," wrote *Super Stock*'s Jim McCraw. "A five-minute stay in any drive-in in any part of the country will be sufficient testament to the car's popularity."

But popularity was one thing, true performance another. Predictably, the 350hp L34 1968 SS 396 was a relatively mild muscle car best suited for performance customers who preferred image over everything else. According to *Motor Trend*, a four-speed L34 could hit 60mph from rest in 7.4 seconds—not earth-shaking, but more than enough to impress your girlfriend. Quarter-mile performance was equally cool: 16 seconds at 89mph for the stick; a slightly quicker 15.8/90 for the Turbo Hydra-matic L34. Letting those figures speak for themselves, *Motor Trend*'s test crew picked out positives like the new, finned front brake drums, which aided cooling, and the

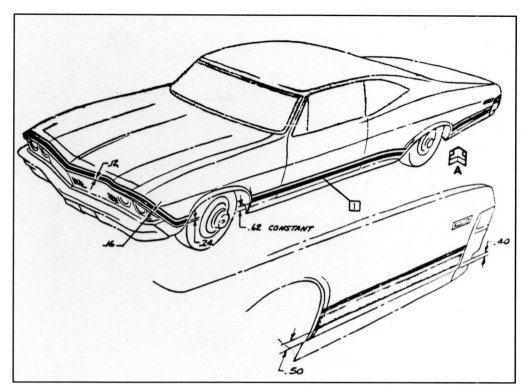

*Available in black, white, or red for Super Sport Chevelles only, the D96 pinstripes* cost $29.50 and were ordered by 18,934 SS 396 buyers in 1968.

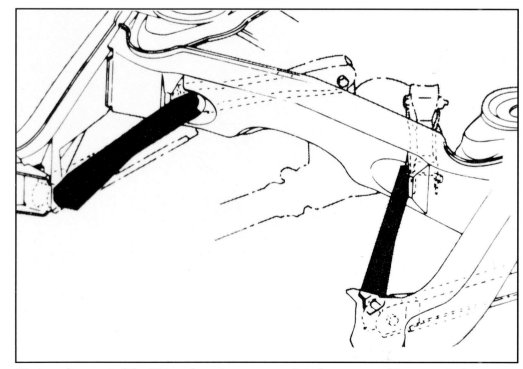

*First used as part of the Z16 package in 1965, these two control arm braces (in black) became standard SS 396 rear suspension equipment from 1966 on. The braces tied together the four mounting* points for upper and lower control arms, negating flex under hard acceleration. Nonetheless, test drivers constantly complained of the SS 396's tendency for wheel hop.

*This 1968 SS 396 convertible shows both the optional D96 pinstripes and the standard Super Sport lower body treatment, which reportedly were never paired together on SS 396s built after December 1, 1967.*

improved, optional metallic brake linings. After warning readers that the metallic brakes "are noisy in the morning (or when cold), and hardly operate at all until warmed up," the *Motor Trend* report then noted, "after that, they hang on like an unemployed relative."

Flogging an L34 SS 396 with a bit more enthusiasm, *Super Stock*'s lead foots managed a best quarter-mile pass of 15 seconds flat, an achievement that still left them disappointed. "If all the 350hp cars are like the one we had," concluded Jim McCraw, "the Chevelle will be in serious trouble on the drag strip." McCraw partially blamed the 1968 L34's deficiencies at the track on the Chevelle rear suspen-

sion, which allowed too much wheel hop under heavy acceleration. He also had a bone to pick with the Muncie shifter, a so-called performance piece that seemingly defied logic.

Muncie's four-speed Chevelle stick had two things working against it. First, its linkage was tied to both the transmission and the frame's transmission cross-member. Once the engine torqued over under high revs, linkage geometry was horribly distorted, making quick, sure shifts almost impossible. To top it off, console-equipped cars encased the shifter arm in a bizarre set of sliding plastic plates that just begged to bind. McCraw called the design "the most Mickey Mouse lashup we've seen. With a gem like that, it was just impossible to keep a smooth flow of power going." His recommendation was to turn to the performance aftermarket: "With enough dollars to buy the car, and a few more for a Hurst shifter and some traction bars and tires, the sharp buyer can make a [1968 L34] work.

But it's a shame the factory didn't do more to uphold the reputation of its hot number."

*Car Life*'s critics agreed wholeheartedly, even after driving the much stronger L78 version. Clearly demonstrating a bias towards more practical, easier to handle transportation, *Car Life* tested both a 375hp SS 396 and a 275hp Malibu, resulting in raves for the sedate small-block Chevelle and a thumbs down for the big-block brute. "We were not impressed with the SS 396. This is America's largest selling Supercar, so it can't be all bad. Still, the overall combination of ride, handling and accelerative performance seemed sub-par in today's Supercar market." Armed with an M21 close-ratio four-speed and 3.55:1 Positraction gears, *Car Life*'s test Chevelle scored a 14.8 in the quarter, maxing out at 98.8mph.

Practically everything about "this rough idling, noisy, gnarly monster" seemingly ticked off the *Car Life* staff, from its nose-heavy handling, to its reported poor fit and finish and "inferior" ride quality, to that "abominable sliding shift lever plate."

*Car Life* continued, "The GM designer responsible for this console slider should have to drive a car equipped with one." If only *Car Life*'s people had told their readers what they really thought...

Perhaps understanding the car's intentions a bit better, *Popular Hot Rodding*'s Lee Kelley demonstrated just how well the sharp buyer could make a 1968 L78 SS 396 work. Like the others, Kelley did have his complaints, the prime one concerning that pesky shifter. "When a hot rodder lays out almost $4,000 for a high-performance machine, he shouldn't have to go out and spend more money to install a decent shifter," he wrote. He was also annoyed by the unusual 1968 tachometer, which used a vertical scale and was deeply recessed in the dash. According to Kelley, it "has to rank among the world's worst. We have one suggestion when considering a tach as optional equipment on the Chevelle. Don't! Buy some reliable tach from your local speed equipment dealer." Kelley also labeled overall quality control as "only fair," and pointed out that the stock F70x14 rubber was typically "no match for this much power." But from there, everything else came up roses.

"Quick, fast and potent," was Kelley's initial description of the 375hp Super Sport. Handling was equally hot in his eyes, as were the optional front disc brakes. "Everyone knows the 375 Chevelle runs good in a straight line, but what really impressed us was its handling. While performance on the road courses fell far short of the sports car crowd, it definitely showed us that it could run with the best of the Detroit offerings. [And] straight-line stopping was fantastic."

Facing the same obstacles put before its rivals among the automotive press, *Popular Hot Rodding* recorded a 15.05/96 best in the quarter-mile on smoky street tires. A set of slicks alone dropped the ET down to 14.30 seconds, then a few passes at higher shift points (upwards of 7000rpm) resulted in a 13.83-second run. Headers helped even more, lowering the L78's ET to 13.60 seconds at 105mph. *Popular Hot*

*Rodding*'s test left Kelley wondering what traction bars and rear gears lower than the 3.55s used would produce. Calling the 1968 375hp SS 396 "a hot contender at the drag strip," he concluded: "Although it is not the fastest machine right off the showroom floor, it does possess much more potential than any other car in its field. With a minimum cash outlay and a lot of elbow grease, this car can be [a] street eliminator any night of the week. Chevy may not be in racing, but its cars sure are!"

As attractive as the 1968 SS 396 was, Super Sport Chevelle production for 1968 dipped slightly to 57,595, a result undoubtedly attributable to the growing population in the muscle car field. Chevrolet's slice of the pie may have decreased, but so, too, did everyone else's, as countless high-powered intermediates, pony cars, and full-sized models rolled out of Detroit.

Along with those 57,595 SS Chevelles, Chevy built 5,190 SS 396 El Caminos in 1968, the first time the Super Sport designation had been applied to the El Camino line. Since 1966, all items and equipment avail-

able to Super Sport Chevelle customers, including the various 396 big-blocks, could be included on Custom El Camino models, with the exception of the Super Sport nomenclature. In 1966 and 1967, "396 Turbo Jet" cross-flags were no strangers to El Camino fenders, but "SS 396" badges were nowhere to be found. Chevrolet officials rectified that injustice in 1968, to the delight of buyers who preferred hard-working high performance, and wanted everyone to know it in no uncertain terms.

"Fancier than a truck, more utilitarian than a passenger car, able to leap past sports cars in a single bound, the [SS 396] El Camino will fill needs the owner never knew he had," or so claimed *Car Life*, which reported an impressive quarter-mile pass of 14.80

*El Caminos finally got the full SS 396 treatment for 1968, the only year an SS 396 El Camino was offered as a specific individual model in its own right. In 1969, the SS 396 features became an optional package, labelled RPO Z25. For 1968, 5,190 SS 396 El Caminos were built.*

*The underhood lineup for the 1968 SS 396 carried over unchanged from 1967, with the 325hp big-block as standard equipment. RPO L78, still a bit difficult to find in official Chevrolet paperwork, remained the top Super Sport powertrain option. Output remained at 375hp at 5600rpm, with maximum torque of 415lb-ft coming at 3600rpm.*

seconds at 94.93mph for a 350hp L34 El Camino Super Sport equipped with the Turbo Hydra-matic automatic and standard 3.31:1 gears. With a little tweaking, *Hot Rod* managed to lower the SS 396 El Camino ante to 14.49/98.79—serious travelling for a machine *Hot Rod*'s Steve Kelly called "the near-perfect 'Gentleman's hauler.'"

As it turned out, 1968 would be the one and only year for the SS 396 El Camino as an individual, distinct model. No, Chevrolet didn't stop building them; the company simply changed the vehicle's designation.

While all SS 396s, Chevelle and El Camino, were listed as their own model series in 1968, the SS 396 became an optional package in 1969, listed as RPO Z25. Offered again on the Custom El Camino, Z25 equipment also found its way onto four different 1969 Chevelle models in a marked departure from existing practices. From 1966 to 1968, the SS 396 was based on either the Malibu sport coupe or convertible. For 1969, RPO Z25 was extended down into the less prestigious 300 ranks as well, becoming available on the 300 Deluxe sport coupe and the 300 Deluxe sedan. Although no production records are available, the 1969 SS 396 300 post sedan is a rare bird indeed.

Priced at $347.60, RPO Z25 was basically the same package offered for 1966 to 1968, with a couple of nice additions thrown in for good measure. Standard power still came from the 325hp 396 backed by a three-speed manual transmission, and the beefed chassis also remained. On top, the SS

hood with its twin bulges carried over, as did the blackout treatment front and rear, with appropriate "SS 396" identification. Inside, the standard bench seat interior again featured "SS" identification on the steering wheel and "SS 396" tags on both the door panels and the dashboard's passenger side (in 1966 and 1967, the dashboard emblem simply read "Super Sport"). At $121.15, Strato-buckets continued as a popular option for the discriminating SS 396 buyer.

Outside, the 1969 Super Sport Chevelle received new "SS 396" emblems on the fenders, items that greatly enhanced the image. The deletion of all the excess lower body clutter, which in 1968 included contrasting black paint, chrome trim delineation, and varying striping treatments, improved the look. Although the 1969 body was essentially identical to the 1968's, overall impressions were noticeably upgraded, thanks mostly to this cleanup. Buyers could add the lower body paint at extra cost, but the

standard paint scheme came off as exceptionally attractive without it. A more suitable choice was the D96 wide upper body accent stripe.

Most prominent among the additions made to the SS 396 standard equipment list for 1969 were power front disc brakes and a set of new SS wheels. Suggested for the SS 396 lineup since their introduction two years before, RPOs J52 and J50 (power assist) were welcome additions, featuring 11in rotors and single-piston calipers in place of the four-piston J52 design used in 1967 and 1968. Set off by chrome wheel opening mouldings, the attractive 14x7 five-spoke JJ rims included small "SS" center caps and bright trim rings. The sporty five-spokes, a notable departure from the dog-dish caps that had been standard SS 396 fare for three years, were the only wheels available for 1969 Super Sports. Chevy's popular Rally wheels were still around in the A-body ranks, but weren't offered on SS 396s.

The transformation of a more mundane 300 model into an SS 396 required a slightly different approach. First, roof rail drip gutters, larger taillight bezels, and the upper body accent stripe were added, as were upper and lower rear cove mouldings. Deleted were the rocker mouldings and the "300 Deluxe" fender script, which was replaced, of course, by the new "SS 396" identification. Inside, the dash and steering wheel both got the SS identification trim treatment, but the 300 door panels didn't. And since only Malibu models featured hideaway windshield wipers, the wiper arms on a 300 SS 396 didn't retract beneath the cowl edge of the twin-bulge Super Sport hood. From there, however, everything else was basic Z25 right down to the sport wheels.

Chevrolet also created a few changes on the options list for 1969, as the 375hp L78 finally got equal billing to the standard 325hp 396 and the $121.15 350hp L34. Priced at $252.50, the L78 396 reached its peak

*Other than the "SS" identification on the steering wheel and new "SS 396" badges on the door panel, the standard 1968 SS 396 interior featured basic Chevelle pieces. On the options list were Strato-buckets, a console, a sport steering wheel, and full instrumentation, which included yet another cleverly hidden tachometer. Deeply recessed in the center between the large square housings for the speedometer and clock, the 1968 tach used a vertical scale to give shift point readouts—and went over like the typical lead balloon. Chevrolet's infamous Muncie shifter was a unit that considerably hindered the 1968 SS 396's performance, according to every automotive journalist who tested one. Attached to both transmission and frame cross-member, the shift linkage tended to bind up under hard acceleration once torque twisted the transmission.*

in popularity, finding its way into 9,486 1969 Chevelles and El Caminos. But the L78 didn't represent the top of the list. New for 1969 was the L89 aluminum head option for the 375hp 396. Offered with Corvettes and Ca-

*"If competition had one like this, we'd have a lot more competition."* By 1969, Chevrolet's SS 396 was Detroit's most popular muscle car, a fact copywriters weren't adverse to noting in the 1969 Chevelle brochure.

maros, too, the lightweight L89 heads trimmed off precious pounds when competition was the intended use. The weight loss, however, didn't come cheap—counting cash put down for the L78, the L89 option totalled

A slight SS 396 revamp made a major difference in 1969. The blacked-out grille up front was more aggressive; a revised roofline made for a lighter look; prominent "SS 396" identification on the fender left little doubt of what you were looking at; and standard five-spoke "SS" wheels completed the image.

$647.75. Some 400 customers reportedly reached deep for the L78/L89 power package in 1969.

Transmission choices for 1969 carried over with two exceptions. First,

the Powerglide automatic was finally deleted from Super Sport ranks, leaving the Turbo Hydra-matic to carry the load alone. Turbo Hydra-matics were also offered behind the brutish L78 for the first time, as were all the manuals, including the Super Sport "special" MC1 three-speed and M20 wide-ratio four-speed, units that previously had been spared the wrath of 375 horses. Meanwhile, the M21 close-ratio four-speed remained exclusive to the 350 and 375hp 396s, and the M22 Rock Crusher was again offered only with the L78.

Standard rear gears ranged from the 325hp 396's 3.07:1 to the L78's 3.55s. Positraction and ratios as low as 4.88:1 were listed at extra cost, with 3.73, 4.10, 4.56, and 4.88 gears delivered in Positraction differentials only. All gear ratios lower than 3.73:1 tacked on an additional $13.75 to the $42.15 Positraction asking price, thanks to the mandatory inclusion of the V01 heavy-duty radiator.

Two other new performance features, both hidden underneath, could be added at extra cost as well. The most noticeable of the two had Bill Sanders singing its praises in *Motor Trend*'s January 1969 issue. "Our fervor was really aroused by the one 1969

*For 1969, SS 396 equipment became an options package, RPO Z25. Along with being offered for the Malibu hardtop and convertible, RPO Z25 could be ordered on either of the low-priced 300 Deluxe models, hardtop or sedan. Including the sedan's B-pillar "post," the 300 Deluxe heritage of this 1969 SS 396 also mandated the inclusion of vent windows, items deleted from Malibu models after 1968. There are no available production breakdowns for the odd post-sedan 1969 SS 396, but the cars are rarely seen—1969 was the only year this combination was available. After toying with fake mag wheelcovers and dull, dog-dish hubcaps, Chevrolet designers finally produced a wheel suitable for the SS 396 image. The 14x7 five-spoke "SS" sport rim became standard equipment for 1969, and was the only wheel available for the SS 396. Malibu models first incorporated hideaway windshield wipers in 1968, but the cheaper 300 models still had standard wipers. Ordering the Z25 option on a 1969 300 Deluxe didn't change this fact, as the exposed wipers on this SS 396 sedan demonstrate.*

Chevrolet addition that is guaranteed to turn you on, or you aren't a red-blooded, hairy-chested American male." Sanders was referring to RPO NC8, the $15.80 chambered dual exhaust system. Basically a set of flow-through pipes with eight sets of eleven baffles running its 45in length (two smaller baffled pipes were included farther back), chambered exhausts were street legal, although any "red-blooded, hairy-chested" peace officer within earshot surely must have questioned that fact. As Sanders explained, "the sound [chambered exhaust] puts out is pure pleasure," but he was "sure that many a local gendarmerie, untuned to such vibrations, will take a different attitude." Chambered exhausts reportedly came standard with the L34 396 before December 1968, when they were transferred to the RPO list. A rare option, NC8 was cancelled May 19, 1969.

*Chrome exhaust tips had become standard SS 396 items in 1968, although apparently not all 1968 SS 396s included them. By 1969, however, all Super Sport Chevelles, 300 Deluxe sedan or Malibu hardtop, came with the bright extensions. This sedan's color, Hugger Orange, was one of two special-order finishes borrowed from the Camaro for SS 396s only in 1969. The other shade was Daytona Yellow. After leaving the fenders essentially blank in 1968, designers chose to promote the SS 396 image more prominently in 1969 with an "SS 396" fender badge.*

The other new addition was the now-legendary F41 sport suspension, which did the existing F40 heavy-duty option one better. Offered to Chevelle buyers since 1964, the F40 suspension simply stiffened the springs and shocks. RPO F41 exchanged the tried-and-true .937in front sway bar for an unflinching 1.125in unit, and added a

*As if a 1969 SS 396 sedan isn't rare enough, this 300 Deluxe is powered by an aluminum-head L78 big-block. The addition of the aluminum heads, RPO L89, didn't change the L78's 375hp output, but it did cut off important pounds for race-minded buyers. Only 400 L89/L78 SS 396s were built in 1969; estimates claim maybe six were of the 300 Deluxe sedan variety.*

.875in rear stabilizer bar along with "special duty" bushings, reinforced lower control arms in back, and beefier springs and shocks all around. The combination of the F41 underpinnings with the standard SS 396 front discs and optional L78 power unquestionably resulted in the supreme Super Sport Chevelle up to that point.

As usual, road testers concluded that the SS 396 was an average straight-line performer in stock trim, although it was again made clear that a few modifications could easily unleash some serious potential. *Hot Cars* magazine's staff found both rear wheel

hop and slippery rubber to be major stumbling blocks as they recorded a decent, yet disappointing, quarter-mile best of 14.7 seconds at 101mph in a 1969 L78 SS 396. Again, stickier treads and traction bars—as well as cool air induction—were recommended as surefire cures.

*Motor Trend* tested a 350hp 1969 SS 396 automatic, resulting in a typically lukewarm 15.4-second quarter with a terminal speed of 92mph. Demonstrating what a gear change could do, *High Performance Cars,* in its *1969 Supercar Annual,* reported a 14.70/96 ET scored by another L34 Chevelle SS, this one armed with a four-speed and the optional 4.10:1 ratio.

A *Car and Driver* test featuring a base 325hp 1969 SS 396 was somewhat amazing. Equipped with the Turbo Hydra-matic trans, F40 suspension, and 3.55 Positraction gears, *Car and Driver*'s Super Sport Chevelle managed an impressive 14.41/97.35 quarter-mile pass. Clearly running

contrary to comparable efforts, these results didn't quite add up, especially when you noted that a 325hp Camaro tested earlier by *Car and Driver* couldn't break 15 seconds in the quarter. Trying to explain its numbers, *Car and Driver*'s staff claimed "that the Chevelle exhaust system is far more efficient than that of the Camaro and the '69 emission control system, which does not use an air injection pump [manual trans SS 396s did], improves output."

Once again, *Car and Driver* picked wheel hop and insufficient rubber as the 396 Chevelle's main drawbacks, although it did conclude that a buyer who shelled out for the 375hp option would "end up with the real thing." For the average Chevelle customer, Chevy's 375hp 396 was as "real" as it got in 1969. But for a select few, even more power was available just one Central Office Production Order (COPO) away.

Shrouded in mystery and only recently recognized, Chevrolet's COPO

427 Chevelles would have had all automotive journalists hanging on for dear life had they been lucky enough to test one back in 1969. Most, however, didn't even know they existed—remember, GM had placed a 400ci limit on all its divisions' intermediates in 1965.

But the COPO pipeline—with a little help from performance projects manager Vince Piggins—provided an easy way around that limit. COPOs were most commonly used for situations like special fleet orders from trucking firms or police departments, where superseding corporate red tape simply made good business sense. Channeled through COPOs, special requests from volume buyers did not require upper management approval; a nod from Chevrolet Engineering was all that was needed. From there, the logic was simple: if it worked for trucks, it could surely do the same for special-duty performance cars.

Inspired by Illinois Chevrolet dealer Fred Gibb and drag racer Dick Harrell, Piggins had begun toying with the idea of using COPOs to build 427 Camaros and Chevelles as early as July 1968, and despite GM's disapproval of a 427 pony car prototype, the three men did manage to unleash the legendary ZL1 all-aluminum 427 Camaro—COPO 9560—in January 1969. Although surely the most exotic of the big-block F-body breed, Gibb's ZL1 Camaro was not alone.

In Canonsburg, Pennsylvania, Don Yenko, another hot-blooded Chevy dealer, had been building and marketing his own 427 Camaros since 1967, transplanting in the more civilized L72 425hp Corvette 427. Having had enough of the troublesome transplants, Yenko inspired the other famed COPO Camaro, 9561, the cast-iron L72 version. There is still some controversy over exactly when Yenko's crew first started taking delivery of factory-equipped L72 Camaros. (Reported evidence of 1968 427 model deliveries is now being investigated, and some believe Yenko may have been the first to discuss a COPO car plan with Piggins.) It is known, however, that Yenko was using the COPO 9561 Camaro as a base for his 427 Super Car by 1969.

Yenko also gets credit for the mysterious COPO Chevelle. After refining

his 427 F-body model, he simply took the same tack in A-body form, ordering a special run of COPO 9562 427 Chevelles later in 1969, converting them into eye-catching, gut-wrenching Yenko SC Chevelles (see the Yenko sidebar, "Over The Limit"). In an interview just before his death in March 1987, Yenko mystifyingly told *Musclecar Review*'s Greg Rager that his SC Chevelles began life as 1969 SS 396s, with L72 427s being transplanted into the cars at his Canonsburg dealership. This claim, undoubtedly the result of a memory lapse of some sort, was simply not correct, as any Yenko Chevelle build sheet will attest—without a doubt, all SC Chevelles were COPO cars. Even though a COPO Chevelle build sheet will include an "L78 375 Turbo Jet" reference, the appropriate 427 engine code, as well as a host of optional codes, tells the true tale.

Once Yenko Sports Cars, Inc., got the ball rolling, other high-performance Chevy outlets like Baldwin-Motion in New York jumped into the 427 Chevelle game, although the Motion Performance cars were apparently all dealer conversions. And since COPO Camaros and Chevelles weren't limit-

*The SS steering wheel and Muncie four-speed shifter seemingly clash with the mundane 300 interior. And since the door panels differed in a Malibu and a 300 Deluxe (due to the 300's vent windows), this Super Sport sedan didn't receive the appropriate "SS 396" door badges.*

ed to dealer purchases, individual customers in the know also got into the act, with the result being an intriguing, somewhat confusing, paper trail of COPO codes and options combos, all aimed at unleashing 427-powered Chevelles onto the street.

There were eight different COPO 9562 combinations available for the model 13637 1969 Chevelle hardtop, each with its own two-letter suffix. Common to all COPO 9562 option groups regardless of the suffix code present was the 425hp L72 427, backed by either an M21 four-speed or M40 Turbo Hydra-matic 400 automatic (the M22 Rock Crusher four-speed was also available). Potent L72 features included 11:1 compression, a solid-lifter cam (.520in lift, 316degree duration intake, 302degree exhaust), big-valve heads (2.19in intakes, 1.72 exhausts), and an 800cfm Holley four-barrel on an aluminum manifold. Torque output was 460lb-ft.

Also listed on the COPO 9562 parts list were the L72's oil pan, left-hand exhaust manifold, and clutch fork assembly and housing, all basic L78 SS 396 components. A requisite heavy-duty radiator was part of the deal as well. Completing the package was a special, heavy-duty 12-bolt Positraction rear end (4.10:1 ratio) with reinforced differential components and casing and a beefed-up ring-and-pinion assembly—not all COPO 9562 rear end parts and SS 396 RPO G80 Positraction pieces would interchange.

With the basic COPO 9562 "High Performance Unit" components established, the eight combinations read as follows:

| COPO # | Description |
|---|---|
| 9562AA | Four-speed manual transmission |
| 9562BA | M40 three-speed automatic transmission |
| 9562CD | Four-speed manual trans, special contour bucket seats, COPO tires, and special order springs |
| 9562CE | Same as 9562CD except excludes special contour bucket seats |
| 9562DD | M40 three-speed automatic trans, special contour bucket seats, COPO tires, and special order springs |
| 9562DE | Same as 9562DD except excludes special contour bucket seats |
| 9562EA | Four-speed manual trans, RPO J52 disc brakes, and RPO L78 tires |
| 9562FA | Same as 9562EA except exchanges M40 three-speed automatic trans for the four-speed manual |

According to a 1969 Chevrolet assembly manual addendum letter, COPOs 9562AA and BA were "used as a *vehicle combination* with [the] COPO option 9694 front disc brake unit." As mentioned, the Super Sport's J52 front discs were also available through COPOs 9562EA and FA, and the COPO 9694 brakes were available in concert with COPO 9737—the Sports Car Conversion—through two different options package codes, which would have been paired up with the COPO 9562 "High Performance Unit." Code 9694CA included the four-speed transmission, the Sports Car Conversion, and power front discs. Code 9694CB was identical, except for the Turbo Hydra-matic in place of the Muncie four-speed.

Specially created for Yenko Sports Cars, from whence it takes its name, COPO 9737 included a heavier front stabilizer bar, 15x7 JJ Rally wheels with hub caps and trim rings, and appropriate speedometer equipment to compensate for the various trans, axle ratio, and wheel and tire combinations.

Listed separately from the eight main options combinations in that same addendum were two more COPO combos, numbers 9566AA and 9566BA. As if there weren't enough codes already, COPO 9566AA was described as "the same as option 9562EA with the exception of tires." COPO 9566BA held the same exception related to the automatic trans code 9562FA. Confused? Don't feel alone.

Once a COPO 9562 customer deciphered all the letter codes, he received an odd combination of maximum big-block power, heavy-duty hardware, Super Sport imagery, and basic Malibu accoutrements. The attractive D96 upper body accent stripe, SS blackout grille and rear cove panel, twin-bulge SS hood, heavy-duty suspension, and chrome exhaust extensions were included, but the car wasn't a Super Sport. Other than "SS" identification on the steering wheel of some cars (not all factory 427 Chevelles came with this feature), no other Super Sport

*This SS steering wheel is the only Super Sport identification showing on this particular 427 Chevelle—the rest of the interior is pure Malibu. Most COPO cars came with standard steering wheels. Although no hard production figures are available, it is known that Chevrolet built ninety-six "MP-code" L72s for Turbo Hydra-matic applications in COPO 9562 Chevelles, compared to 277 427/four-speed combos, coded "MQ." These figures are for engines built, not models produced.*

76

tions, most 427 Chevelles rolled on 15in Rallys. Fourteen-inch Rallys were available for regular-production Chevelles in 1969, but for Malibus, not Super Sports, which came with only one type of wheel, the exclusive 14x7 five-spoke SS rim. Comparable in appearance to the 1968 Corvette 15x7 Rally wheel (for 1969, Corvette dimensions increased to 15x8), the JJ rims used with COPO 9562 actually differed slightly in offset from their Corvette counterparts, and carried an appropriate option code all their own (YH, instead of the Corvette's AG).

Some COPO Chevelles, however, did mount the typical 1969 Super Sport 14x7 wheels. COPO code numbers 9562AA and 9562BA didn't list any special wheel/tire combination as part of the package, meaning that these cars were probably equipped with the standard Super Sport wheels unless superseded by another option or options group. Optional "COPO Tires," RPO #ZP1, were available, and probably would have included the larger Rally wheels, since ZP1 rubber measured 15in. ZP1 tires were four-ply Goodyear Polyglas F70-15s embossed with "Goodyear Wide Tread GT" in raised white letters, and apparently were never used on any other Chevrolet product.

COPO codes 9562CD, CE, DD, and DE automatically included the 15in Goodyear Wide Treads and thus the Rally wheels as well, while COPOs 9562EA and FA listed the "RPO L78 tires," F70-14s with their smaller SS wheels. And for those who successfully made heads or tails out of the COPO code jungle, the 15in Rally wheels and Goodyear Wide Treads could have been obtained by checking off COPO 9737, the Sports Car Conversion, just as Don Yenko did for his SC Chevelles.

With or without modifications made by performance dealers like Yenko, the COPO Chevelle was one tough customer. As mentioned, the automotive press missed its chance to test a box-stock 1969 COPO Chevelle—or at least nothing was printed about it in 1969. Twenty years later, veteran performance reporter Roger Huntington finally tapped out a story for *Musclecars* magazine detailing a

*With no identification showing whatsoever, the 425hp L72 Corvette 427 V-8, installed in the 1969 COPO 9562 Chevelle, could have easily passed for a tamer 396. Comparable in compression (11:1) to the 375hp L78 396, the L72 427 featured a .520in lift, solid-lifter cam; free-breathing heads; and a large, 800cfm Holley four-barrel. According to Tonawanda assembly plant records, 373 L72s were assembled for the COPO 9562 application.*

nomenclature was present inside or out—COPO 9562 even specifically replaced the "SS 396" grille emblem with the basic Chevelle Bow-Tie—and nowhere was the 427's presence given away by an emblem or decal, not even under the hood.

Adding more confusion were the wheels used on COPO 9562 cars. Contrary to 1969 SS 396 specifica-

COPO Chevelle he had come across while testing a ZL1 Camaro for *Cars Illustrated* back in May 1969. Huntington called it "the ultimate sleeper" because of its plain-Jane exterior and, interestingly, its set of 15x6 stock-steel rims with hubcaps. Tires were the basic COPO items, F70 Goodyear Wide Tread GTs, and a Turbo Hydra-matic 400 backed up the L72.

For his *Musclecars* article, Huntington managed to dig up twenty-year-old time slips for the car, the best one in stock trim reading 13.82 seconds at 101.45mph. After a few modifications—wider F60 rubber, double-stacked 14x3 air filters, bigger exhaust pipes with less-restrictive mufflers, and a few shift point tweaks in the Turbo 400—those numbers were lowered to 13.42 at 106.21mph. *Super Stock and Drag Illustrated* put a Yenko Chevelle through its paces at about the same time, producing a best ET of 13.31/108.04. Either way, a 427 Chevelle ranked among Detroit's hottest factory stock offerings.

No one is one hundred percent sure how many 1969 COPO Chevelles were built, although it is known that Yenko Chevrolet was the number one customer. Documenting this strange machine is not easy, as records don't specifically mention the 427 A-body application. But according to Tonawanda engine plant employee and Chevy big-block expert Fran Preve, possible answers can be found in factory paperwork. Engine production records for 1969 show that Chevrolet built 277 L72 427s for manual transmission COPO 9562 applications (code MQ), along with ninety-six M40 Turbo Hydra-matic-backed COPO 427s (code MP), for a total of 373 powertrain combos. This figure represents total engines produced, not cars built. Relying on a little speculation, Preve has estimated that perhaps as many as 323 COPO Chevelles were built, with at least ninety-nine of those going to Yenko Chevrolet. Preve does point out that while this figure is not a documented fact, it probably comes a lot closer to the truth than other production claims ranging from 100 to 500 and even 1,000.

Any way you look at it, the COPO Chevelle is a mystery, having come

and gone in 1969 before most super car fans knew what had transpired. One year later, GM's 400ci limit would fall by the wayside, allowing the big bully 454ci Mk IV to make its A-body debut and eliminating any need to fuss with COPOs and 427s. And as the 1969 model year was winding down, engineers bored out the veteran 396 big-block by a measly .032in, resulting in another jump over the displacement limit just before it came down. Not wanting to rock the boat nor break something that didn't need fixing, Chevy officials would stick with the "SS 396" image even though the new engine actually displaced 402 cubes.

SS 396 production reached its peak in 1969, numbering 86,307 for both Chevelles and El Caminos. Although it was certainly a great year for Super Sport Chevelles, the true performance pinnacle was still ahead.

*Somewhat of an enigma, the 1969 COPO Chevelle featured various SS 396 exterior pieces, but the car wasn't a Super Sport. Present is the SS 396's hood, grille, blacked-out rear cove, dual chrome exhaust tips, and optional D96 bodyside stripe. The 15x7 Rally wheels, however, are unique to the COPO Chevelle. Slightly incorrect, the tires should include the words "Wide Tread" in white letters.*

*Following pages*
*Even though Chevrolet couldn't officially offer a 427 Chevelle in 1969, thanks to GM's edict limiting A-bodies to 400ci, performance guru Vince Piggins could still use the Central Office Production Order (COPO) pipeline to circumvent existing red tape. The result was the COPO Chevelle powered by the Corvette's 425hp 427 Mk IV big-block, RPO L72. Low-13-second screamers, COPO Chevelles could be equipped with either the Turbo Hydra-matic automatic or the M21 four-speed. The M22 "Rock Crusher" four-speed was also available.*

viewers then posed the question "does it do any good?" Not in their minds. "Possibly the cold air inducted at the base of the windshield would be helpful at very high speeds, but a similar Chevelle SS 396 without Cowl Induction ran essentially the same speeds. It's a gimmick, but sometimes people need fun little gimmicks." *Car Life's* testers basically agreed, claiming the ZL2 hood "probably adds some power, and kids love it." As they say, image is everything.

In the case of the '70 SS 396, imagery was very important, as were overall impressions. Chevrolet's SS 396 didn't become one of Detroit's most popular muscle cars on sheer brute force alone; on the contrary, the majority of the 396 Chevelles were average straight-line performers, as was the basic 350hp 1970 rendition. Best quarter-mile times registered in the low 15s at barely 90 mph—fast, but not serious super car stuff as most automotive magazines once more pointed out.

Then again, defining a super car represented an entirely different story from the perspective of the average customer, who probably needed to drive his vehicle a bit more than a quarter-mile at a time. Sure, SS 396 performance could have been maxed out with a host of high-priced, hard-to-live-with, hot hardware, but the trade-offs were obvious. When it came to uncompromised everyday operation, few super cars could match the '70 SS 396's nicely balanced combination of handling, braking, ride, comfort, pizzazz, and, yes, performance.

As *Car Life* proclaimed leading off a '70 SS 396 road test, "The best-selling Supercar isn't the quickest. But it looks tough. And it's kind to women and children"—kind because this car wasn't a cramped, cantankerous beast, it was a real driver for real people with, perhaps, real families. "Adults can ride in the rear seat, as they should be able to in a car of this size," read the *Car Life* report. "With the handling package, brakes, etc., the SS 396 makes a fine family car."

"The Chevelle SS 396 has been a very fine seller and it is not difficult to see why," echoed *Road Test*. "It has strong youth appeal but Chevrolet management feels that it is beginning

*In 1970, the SS Chevelle received an exclusive dashboard layout for the first time, although its three-pod arrangement was basically borrowed from the Monte Carlo. Options appearing here include*

*Strato-buckets and console, M21 four-speed, full instrumentation with tachometer, air conditioning, and a sport steering wheel with tilt column.*

*Although Super Sport El Caminos did receive "SS" steering wheel identification, they didn't get the "SS 396" door panel emblems for much the same reasons the 1969 SS 396 300 sedan didn't—both*

*vehicles had vent windows which the Malibu-based Super Sports did not, meaning that a different inner door panel was used, negating the use of the appropriate emblem.*

*Previous pages*
*The king of kings, the 1970 LS6 SS 454—in convertible form, no less. Total LS6 production for Malibu hardtops and convertibles and Custom El Caminos in 1970 was 4,475; estimates put LS6 convertible production at somewhere between twenty and seventy-five. LS6 Chevelles were among Detroit's fastest factory hot rods, reaching the low thirteens in the quarter-mile. Breaking into the 12-second bracket required very little sweat.*

*Below*
*For the first time since 1965, a different displacement engine option became available for the 1970 Super Sport Chevelle. Along with the standby "396" Turbo Jet Z25 package came RPO Z15, offering two 454 Mk IV big-blocks, the 360hp LS5 and the truly awesome 450hp LS6. Total SS 454 production for 1970 was 8,773. The plain-Jane hood on this LS6 convertible is indeed an oddity; most cars at least had the D88 "Band-Aid" stripes, and the ZL2 Cowl Induction option was ordered 28,888 times by Chevelle SS and El Camino SS buyers in 1970.*

to be noticed by a much older segment of the buying public. It is a car that can put a little excitement into the life of a jaded motorist without making him look a total hot rodder."

In defense of SS 396 performance, *Road Test* once more picked on inadequate rubber as a reason behind a relatively slow 15.27-second ET, and also mentioned was the '70 Chevelle's heftiness; fully optioned, the car weighed in at roughly 4,100lb. Yet even with all that weight, *Road Test*'s crew felt the car handled great and stopped like a champ. "Deceleration now matches anything of its size at a best stop from 60 mph of 24-26 ft. per sec.$^2$ or about 150 ft. Overall we were very pleased with the car; its performance, handling and comfort we found quite satisfying. It's not a perfect car but it's a good one."

In conclusion, *Car Life* made the most important point. "As the politician-peddler says, it isn't what you are, it's what projects [translated,

image is everything]. The Chevelle Super Sport 396 projects. While Ford rules NASCAR and Plymouth concentrates on the drags, the Chevelle moves out of showrooms everywhere." And wasn't that the idea?

Chevrolet's SS Chevelle sold as well as any other super car of 1970 basically because it looked the part of a super car and it was a *complete* performance package from top to bottom. "You cannot buy the hottest engine without also buying the suspension, tires and brakes that Chevrolet engineers have learned work best," explained *Road Test*. "Some manufacturers sell super cars with minimal suspension and brakes, assuming customers plan to go drag racing where such items matter little or will be altered. It's not such a hot idea to trust a customer that far. At Chevrolet they assume the customer can remove what he doesn't want for racing."

They also assumed that not all Chevelle customers would be satisfied

with a performance vehicle that was "kind to women and children." Although the concept of a fast family car was certainly intriguing, the youth market wasn't dead yet, and many hot-blooded buyers, with or without families, still preferred their performance in all or nothing fashion. For these guys, nothing short of true super car status would do—no compromises, no worries about civility, no expenses spared. In Chevrolet terms the 1970 LS6 Chevelle was all this and more, a super car if there ever was one, ranking right up with the toughest muscle cars ever unleashed on the street.

GM's 400ci limit for its intermediate models was history by 1970, allowing RPO LS6 to appear as a Chevelle SS option. RPO LS6 was the awesome 450hp 454, the supreme evolution of the Mk IV big-block V-8. Other than the LS6's 455ci cousin in Buick-Olds-Pontiac ranks, there was no bigger super car powerplant in 1970, and no

engine in intermediate ranks ever carried a higher advertised output rating. Unlike many earlier performance V-8s that were rated far beyond reality, Chevrolet's LS6 big-block was no baloney; in fact, 450hp was probably a bit on the conservative side.

The LS6 was one of two big 454s offered in 1970 as part of RPO Z15, the SS 454 package for Custom El Caminos and Malibu hardtops and convertibles. Essentially identical to RPO Z25 with the obvious exception of its pumped-up power source, Z15 equipment carried a slightly heftier price tag at $503.45. In base form, an SS 454 '70 Chevelle featured the milder 360hp LS5 Mk IV big-block backed either by the M21 four-speed or M40 Turbo Hydra-matic 400. Moving up to the LS6 bumped the price even higher as the 450hp Turbo-Jet 454 tacked on another $263.30. Mandatory options included a $15.80 heavy-duty battery and a choice between the beefy M22 Rock Crusher

*Three different air cleaners were used on the LS6 454, with this dual-snorkel unit being the rarest. The typical open-element air cleaner was also used in the absence of the ZL2 hood. With the Cowl Induction hood installed, the LS6 was crowned by a single-snorkel air cleaner fitted, of course, with the large rubber doughnut required to seal the unit to the hood's underside. The LS6's 450hp output rating was the highest ever to hit the street—from Chevrolet or from any other auto maker. Torque output was a whopping 500lb-ft at 3600rpm, same as the LS5, but at 400rpm higher.*

four-speed, priced at $221.81, and the $290.40 M40 Turbo 400 automatic. Totalled up, the LS6 option added $1,004.36 to an A-body sticker when the four-speed was ordered, $1,072.95 for the automatic-backed version.

By late summer 1969, everyone and their uncle knew GM's 400ci limit was coming down and Chevrolet's 454 big-block was on its way; exactly when it would officially arrive was the only

*The LS6's closed-chamber heads featured large rectangular ports and big valves,* *2.19in intakes and 1.88in exhausts. Combustion chamber volume was 108cc.*

question. Chevelle brochures announced the SS 454 option right along with all the other new model news, although a disclaimer was included: "Availability may be limited at beginning of 1970 model year; consult your dealer for delivery information." Apparently, regular production began in January 1970, even though magazines like *Car Craft, Car and Driver,* and *Motor Trend* got to test a 450hp Chevelle late in 1969. As *Car and Driver* explained, "there were engines and there were cars—it was just a matter of putting the two together."

Put together with care at Chevrolet's big-block V-8 production plant in Tonawanda, New York, the LS6 454 was specially built from oil pan to air cleaner with real super car performance in mind. Unlike the LS5, which was based on a two-bolt main bearing block, the LS6's bottom end was held together with four-bolt main bearing caps, and the block itself featured pre-tapped holes for a race-minded external oiling system.

*Like its relatively barren exterior, this LS6's interior is also devoid of options—no instrumentation, no Strato-buckets, no console. Just the standard SS steering wheel and a Muncie four-speed stick.*

The LS6 crank was a tuftrided, forged 5140 alloy steel piece cross-drilled to insure ample oil supply to the connecting rod bearings. Rods were forged steel, magnafluxed for rigidity, with 7/16in bolts, as opposed to the LS5's 3/8in units. At the rods' business ends were TRW forged aluminum pistons which mashed the mixture at a ratio of 11.25:1, compared to the LS5's 10.25:1 compression ratio. A .520in lift, 316-degree duration solid-lifter cam took care of valve timing chores, putting the squeeze on 16 sets of heavy-duty dual valve springs through 3/8in diameter pushrods.

LS6 closed-chamber heads breathed with the best of them thanks to large rectangular ports and big valves—2.19in intakes, 1.88in on the exhaust end—but exhaust manifolds were typical low-performance Mk IV items. On the intake side, a Holley 780cfm four-barrel on a low-rise, aluminum manifold fed the beast. Supplying the spark was a typical Mk IV big-block distributor with beefier internals. Deep-groove accessory pulleys completed the LS6 underhood package, perhaps Detroit's greatest performance grouping of all time.

*Car Life* considered the LS6 to be "the best supercar engine ever released by General Motors... Its eccen-

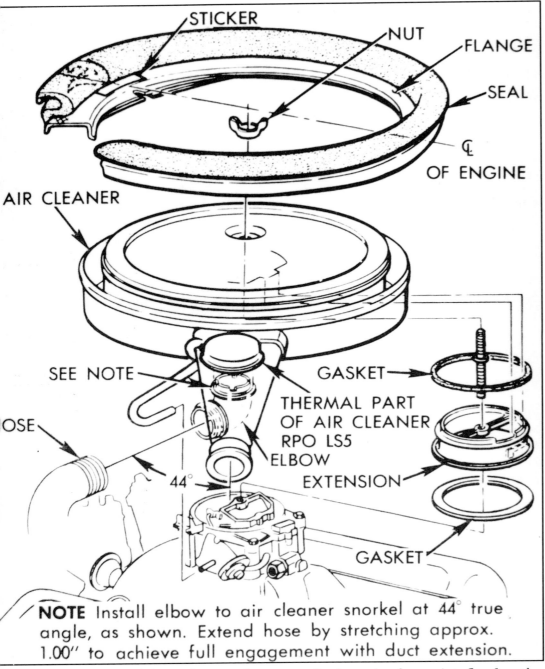

STICKER

NUT

FLANGE

SEAL

C̸L OF ENGINE

AIR CLEANER

SEE NOTE

OSE

GASKET

THERMAL PART OF AIR CLEANER RPO LS5 ELBOW

44°

EXTENSION

GASKET

**NOTE** Install elbow to air cleaner snorkel at 44° true angle, as shown. Extend hose by stretching approx. 1.00" to achieve full engagement with duct extension.

*This design sealed the air cleaner to the underside of the ZL2 Cowl Induction hood,* *allowing cooler, denser air to flow from the base of the windshield into the carburetor.*

tricities are harmless. The solid lifters clatter like Earthquake Day at the canning works, and starting from cold takes many, many cranks of the starter. But the idle is smooth, the top of the rev range relaxed."

*Super Stock* claimed "driving a 450hp Chevelle is like being the guy who's in charge of triggering atom bomb tests. You have the power, you know you have the power, and you know if you use the power, bad things may happen. Things like arrest, prosecution, loss of license, broken pieces, shredded tires, etc. The temptation is always there." *Motor Trend*'s A. B. Shuman came to a similar conclusion, associating the LS6 with a more suit-

able venue. "That's LS as in Land Speed Record."

With 3.31:1 Positraction gears and the Turbo 400 transmission, Shuman's *Motor Trend* test Chevelle ran 0-60 in six seconds and turned a 13.8-second quarter-mile at 97.5mph—with two people along for the ride. Driving a similarly equipped, heavily optioned LS6 '70 Chevelle, *Car and Driver*'s track testers lowered the 0-60 time to 5.4 seconds and upped the terminal speed to 103.80mph after running a nearly identical 13.81-second quarter.

*Super Stock* recorded some serious numbers using a four-speed LS6 equipped with 4.10:1 Positraction gears, as well as the California-mandated smog equipment. Optional in the other forty-nine states, RPO NA9 added an evaporative emission control system that routed fumes from the fuel tank into the carburetor on all California-bound Chevelles. *Super Stock* made special mention of the NA9 equipment so readers "could see why the 450hp engine has breathing problems. Besides all that, the whole mess weighs considerable, and takes up needed space under the hood." But even with NA9, the LS6 was still "a brute... With these pieces to play with, a lot of guys are going to have a lot of SS 454s in the winner's circle this year."

Shifting at upwards of 6800rpm, *Super Stock*'s hot shoes scored consistent ETs in the 13.20-second range at more than 106mph, apparently maximizing the car's ability in stock trim. "It looked like 13.20s were the limit with street rubber. But fear you not. That kind of performance from a 3,800 lb., California-smog-equipped car is very, very good. Given time, a shifter, and tires, a Chevelle SS 454 will make big dents in the 12s."

*Car Craft*'s crew almost made that dent, scoring a 13.12/107.01 ET with a four-speed LS6 Chevelle driven by 3.55:1 Positraction gears. "The car is probably capable of running 13.0s or better with speeds of 108-110 in pure stock form," claimed *Car Craft*'s November 1969 report. "With good tires and some suspension work the mid-12s should be no sweat."

Earlier, *Super Stock* had taken one of the pre-production LS6 press cars with the Turbo 400 transmission and 4.10:1 Positraction gears, added headers and 10.50x15 Goodyear slicks, then proceeded to smoke a 12.69/113.26 quarter-mile pass—"with our photographer driving, yet." Concluded *Super Stock*'s October 1969 report, "the big engine has just got it."

But the big engine didn't have it for long. Granted, 1970 was a pinnacle year for performance, and Chevrolet's LS6 Chevelle was tire-smoking proof. But the term "pinnacle" indicates an ensuing downturn, and 1971 fit that bill. One year after Chevrolet's greatest super car performance, the LS6 Chevelle was history, although it was initially advertised in 425hp form for '71. Doing the LS6 SS 454 in were growing safety concerns among federal legislators and skyrocketing insurance rates, with a little help from tightening emissions standards.

Basically blaming rising insurance costs, an article in *Popular Hot Rodding*'s June 1970 issue written by Roger Huntington and Lee Kelley asked the question, "will there be any '71 super cars?" Reporting rapid rate increases for performance car owners as high as 50 percent, Huntington and Kelley pointed out that "insurance rates are slowly strangling high-performance factory cars today." Average costs to insure a muscle car had gone up about $200 over a six month span early in the year, and it was predicted that a young man under the age of 25 would be paying as much as $500 yearly to insure "a late factory super car" by the end of 1970.

Emissions controls also entered into the picture. To help reduce smog, lower compression ratios and the switch to unleaded gasoline were planned for 1971. Titling its review of Chevrolet's LS6 Chevelle "Last Of The Line," *Car Life* reported gloomy tidings ahead in its September 1970 issue: "At this writing, General Motors' detailed plans for 1971 are still secret. We do know high-compression engines will be dropped, to be replaced by performance engines detuned to use unleaded gasoline. Power will go down. Engines aren't going to get bigger, because emissions controls will soon be based on exhaust volume. Cars won't get lighter, because of safety standards."

In conclusion, *Car Life* called the 450hp SS 454 "something of a high point in Supercars, using the original definition of an intermediate with a big, powerful engine. Without even raising the specters of insurance and social justice, it's fair to say that the Supercar as we know it may have gone as far as it's going."

Answering their question about '71 super cars, Huntington and Kelley remained somewhat optimistic. "There certainly won't be anything available off the showroom floor to compare with what we know today as a super car, but the potential will still be there." Claiming that performance buyers would simply shift their attentions to modifications and mixing and matching parts, *Popular Hot Rodding*'s reporters concluded, "hot rodding isn't dead; on the contrary, it has just been reborn." Four or five years later, while Huntington and Kelley were reading everything they always wanted to know about Vega hop-ups and wild van conversions in *Car Craft*, they probably realized their call was a bit off the mark.

Although the Chevelle SS tale would continue for 1971, the story's end was not far off.

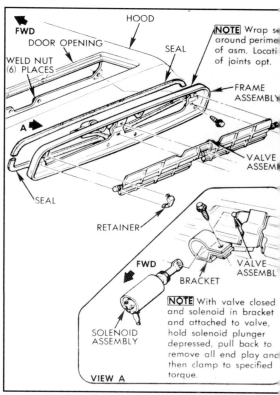

*The business end of the RPO ZL2—this solenoid-operated flap inside the Cowl Induction hood's upper bulge allowed the fresh air to flow once the hammer went down.*

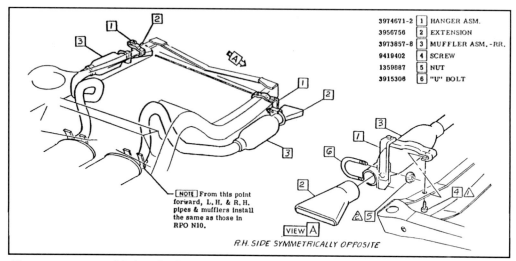

*Resonators were added to the Super Sport's dual exhaust system in 1970.*

# Chapter 7

# 1971–1972

## *End of the Road*

"The commanding lead Chevrolet once held over all other car makers in the horsepower numbers game is over, if not permanently, at least for the forseeable future."
—*Super Stock* Magazine

W hat a difference a year can make. In 1970, Chevrolet's promotional people had been pumping performance like nobody's business, and why not? Super Sport Chevelles for 1970 were among Detroit's hottest products, especially in dominating LS6 trim. But that was then; this was 1971. Almost overnight, federal agencies effectively pulled the plug on horsepower, primarily through escalating emissions

*Opposite*
*Single headlamps borrowed from the Monte Carlo side of the A-body family, and larger 15x7 sport wheels, themselves taken from the Camaro parts bin, set the 1971 SS Chevelle apart from the 1970. Like the 14in, five-spoke SS wheel for 1969 and 1970, the 15in Camaro rim was the only wheel available for 1971 Super Sports. Wider F60 rubber was also new as standard Super Sport equipment for 1971, a fact admen played up big time since they had seemingly little else to talk about. Notice the plain "SS" fender emblem with no engine identification—this Chevelle is equipped with the Turbo Jet 400 big-block. One Super Sport tradition that carried on without change into 1971 was the blacked-out grille with "SS" identification boldly displayed in the center.*

*Unless you ordered the big LS5 454, 1971 Super Sport Chevelles simply carried "SS" emblems on the fenders. Unlike in 1970, when two different SS options packages were listed—RPO Z15 for the 454 and Z25 for the 402—either big-block V-8 was available as part of the single RPO Z15 code in 1971. Missing in this photo are the standard chrome exhaust extensions included with all 1971 big-block SS Chevelles.*

standards. Once only a hassle for hot-car buyers in environmentally conscious California, specialized smog equipment slowly found its way under the hoods of cars sold in all states.

The worst, however, was still to come. Although the various air injection systems and evaporative recovery devices had taken a noticeable toll on performance by 1971, they had by no means strangled the life out of the super car. At least not yet. Having more of an impact at the time were tighter federal emissions standards ahead. Late in 1969, Washington had proposed that even stricter limits be put in place by 1975, limits engineers could only meet through the use of catalytic converter exhaust systems. And since leaded gasoline and catalytic converters don't mix, the switch to unleaded fuel was a foregone conclusion. Recognizing that a complete transformation would take some time, the auto industry began the unleaded era in 1971.

The first step on the way to meeting the 1975 standards was to lower compression. In the summer of 1970 it was announced that more than ninety percent of Detroit's upcoming 1971 models would feature compression ratios low enough to run on 91octane, low-lead fuels. Translated into GM terms, this meant a 9:1 maximum limit, an alarming drop from the head-cracking levels of 1970. What did this mean to Chevelle SS customers?

Initially, it appeared that very little would change despite the lowered compression levels. Early reports in the fall of 1970 listed all powertrain teams as 1971 carryovers, including the awesome LS6 454. With the man-

*A former GM executive's company car, this 1971 SS convertible is fully loaded from nose to tail. Options represented here include Turbo Hydra-matic automatic transmission, Strato-buckets with console,* *tilt wheel, power steering, power door locks (oddly without power windows), rear window defogger, air conditioning, and AM/FM radio.*

*Small-block V-8s returned to the Chevelle SS lineup in 1971, although you'd never know it by looking. Since only the 454-equipped Super Sports carried exterior identification, there was no telling at a glance whether the 1971 Chevelle SS was powered by one of the two available 350ci small-blocks or by the 402 big-block, which was labelled a "Turbo Jet 400." Beneath the Cowl Induction hood on this 1971 SS convertible is the 270hp 350, RPO L48. Although the ZL2 hood option was supposedly limited to big-block Chevelles, various dealers were known to make the installation themselves.*

dated 9:1 compression, the 1971 LS6 was advertised in Chevrolet paperwork at 425hp, still a formidable force. "Even with [less] compression," wrote Roger Huntington in *Popular Hot Rodding*, "this engine will be a strong street performer." Huntington's claim might have stood up, had the 1971 LS6 Chevelle made it out to the street.

Both *Hi-Performance Cars* and *Motor Trend* published road tests of a 1971 LS6 SS 454. In its October 1970 issue, *Motor Trend* reported a diminished quarter-mile time of 14.7 seconds at 89.5mph for a 425hp LS6 Chevelle with standard 3.31:1 gears. According to *Hi-Performance Cars'* *Supercar Annual*, a switch to the optional 4.10:1 Positraction axle helped considerably, lowering the LS6's ET to a more respectable 13.65/102. Interesting numbers, but useless to readers, since the LS6 Chevelle was never officially released for 1971.

As late as January 1971, Chevelle and El Camino options lists included

the LS6 Mk IV V-8, but with a "will advise" note printed in place of a price. According to Chevrolet big-block historian Fran Preve, Tonawanda built a mere fourteen 425hp 454s for A-body applications in 1971, with none of these engines ever making it into a Chevelle sold to the public. Undoubtedly, the magazines' test cars were early mules prepared especially for the press, much like the 1970 LS6 Chevelles that made the magazine rounds prior to the beginning of regular production in late 1969. If any other 1971 LS6 Chevelles escaped into private hands, they remain unknown to this day.

Why the tease? In late 1970 it was clear the days were numbered for true super cars; Chevrolet simply tried to hang on with its top-dog LS6 Chevelle as long as it could. One determining factor that couldn't be denied, however, was the rise in insurance rates. Most insurance companies piled on the premiums relative to a super car's power-to-weight ratio, and not even a

A rose by any other name? In late 1969, engineers had added a slight overbore to the Mk IV big-block V-8, transforming the venerable 396 into a 402. For 1970, decals and factory literature continued to refer to the 396 despite the enlarged displacement. Then, in 1971, the water was truly muddied with the appearance of the "Turbo Jet 400," the same 402ci big-block that had been called a 396 the year before. Although appropriate air cleaner decals for the Turbo Jet 400 were reportedly standard equipment, you will find many 1971 big-block SS Chevelles without them, and the same applies to 1972s. Notice the Cowl Induction underhood ductwork.

reduction to 425hp was going to help a 454 Chevelle customer handle the burden. Stomaching the $1,000 or so for the LS6 package was tough enough; prospective insurance costs wilted many a would-be buyer in his tracks. Times had obviously changed.

Chevrolet's new advertising campaign for 1971 reflected this change. Early in the model year, *Hot Rod* began running a rambling, multi-page presentation detailing Chevy's adjusted attitude. For 1970, one clever picture had been worth thousands of words; a year later, after nearly a thousand words, many prospective buyers still didn't get the picture.

"Driving," began the ad. "Today, it takes in just about everything from the law to your health. It just isn't what it used to be. Ten years ago, there were only two ways to drive American cars. Slow and fast. Now there's another one. Fun." To many, this approach smacked of being told your blind date has a great personality. What exactly did "fun" mean, anyway? Apparently it equalled something called "real driving—just enough of everything, and not too much of anything."

Clearly, Chevrolet's admen were softening up their market in preparation for the inevitable, playing up handling characteristics and performance imagery in an attempt to mask the fact that true performance was on the wane. According to advertisements, the days of going "out to the nearest stretch of highway to prove to some guy that your foot is heavier than his" were over. Almost. Though tamed considerably, Super Sport Chevelles still had a thing or two left to prove.

Unlike in 1970, when two separate Super Sport options packages were offered for the 402 and 454 big-blocks, only one SS equipment group was listed for 1971, labelled RPO Z15 regardless of which engine was installed. Priced at $357, RPO Z15 again included power front disc brakes, F41 sport suspension with rear stabilizer bar, black-accented grille, the impressive domed hood, special instrument panel, "SS" identification, and bright wheel opening trim. New for 1971 as standard Super Sport fare were a remote-control left-hand mirror and racing-style hood pins, which in 1970 were added once the ZL2 Cowl Induction option was ordered. Both RPO ZL2 and the eye-catching D88 "Band-Aid" sport stripes carried over from 1970 on the options list.

Chevelle Super Sports lost their blacked-out rear end treatment thanks to the 1971 Chevelle's restyled rear bumper, which nearly completely covered the tail in chrome. Incorporating a pair of large round taillights at each end, the big bumper carried the appro-priate "SS" badge when RPO Z15 was checked off. Up front, another familiar "SS" emblem was again mounted in the center of the grille, which was also revamped to complement the new 1971 single headlamp setup. Between the grille and rear bumper, 1971 Chevelle sheet metal remained identical to 1970's.

Along with the reshuffled nose and tail, the most noticeable changes in the Super Sport package came at the

*Buyers looking for a tried-and-true SS 396 in 1971 ended up with this engine, RPO LS3, the Turbo Jet 400, a big-block that debuted in 1970 as a non-SS Chevelle option. Actually displacing 402ci, the LS3 was basically a 396 with an enlarged bore and a confusing name. With compression lowered to 8.5:1, the LS3 rated at 300hp. Chrome valve covers, an SS 396 tradition from the start, were exchanged for painted units on the LS3 Turbo Jet 400.*

*Not since 1965 had a small-block V-8 been available to Chevelle SS buyers. In 1971 there were two: this 270hp 350, RPO L48; and the L65 245hp 350. The L65's two-barrel carburetor was another throwback to the days before the SS 396 (the L48 used a four-barrel), as was the single exhaust of both small-blocks, features never offered with the potent big-blocks.*

corners, where 15x7 five-spoke Camaro sport wheels wearing F60 rubber replaced the smaller 14x7 SS wheels used in 1969 and 1970. Like its smaller SS predecessor, the silver-black 1971 Super Sport rim was the only wheel available when RPO Z15 was added to an El Camino or Malibu hardtop or convertible. Most will agree that the increase to 15in represented a marked improvement for the Chevelle SS image.

The Chevelle Super Sport image took somewhat of a fall under the hood, where a small-block V-8 returned as an SS power choice for the first time since 1965. Powerplant choices for 1971 numbered four: two 350ci small-blocks, two Mk IV big-blocks; the LS3 Turbo-Jet 400 (which actually displaced 402ci); and the top-of-the-heap LS5 454. Gone was the revered SS 396 nameplate. Unless you ordered the LS5, 1971 Chevelle Super Sport fend-

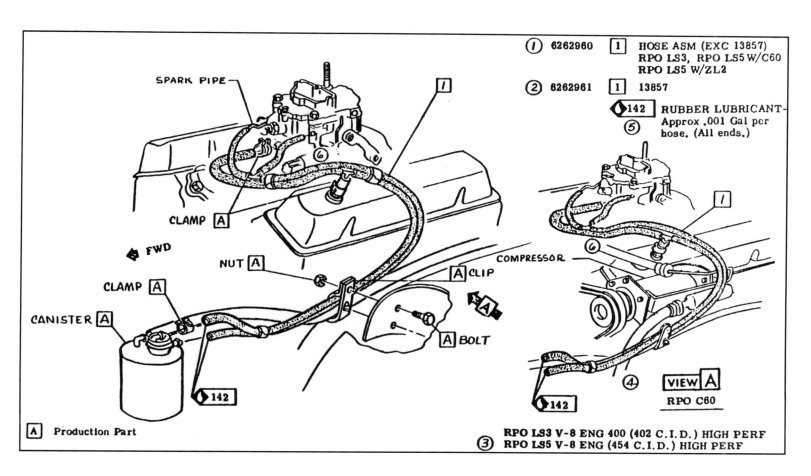

| | | | |
|---|---|---|---|
| ① 6262960 | 1 | HOSE ASM (EXC 13857) RPO LS3, RPO LS5 W/C60 RPO LS5 W/ZL2 | |
| ② 6262961 | 1 | 13857 | |
| ◆142 ⑤ | | RUBBER LUBRICANT-Approx .001 Gal per hose. (All ends.) | |

SPARK PIPE

CLAMP A

◆ FWD

NUT A

CLAMP A

CANISTER A

◆142

COMPRESSOR

A CLIP

A

A BOLT

④ VIEW A
RPO C60

A Production Part

③ RPO LS3 V-8 ENG 400 (402 C.I.D.) HIGH PERF
RPO LS5 V-8 ENG (454 C.I.D.) HIGH PERF

ers were adorned simply with "SS" emblems, whether a small-block or big-block was present inside. LS5 cars, of course, got "SS 454" fender badges. Reportedly, the ZL2 Cowl Induction hood could be ordered only with the two big-blocks, although dealer installations on small-block 1971 Super Sports were apparently performed.

Rated at 245hp, the L65 350ci small-block featured 8.5:1 compression and two other items Chevelle Super Sport buyers hadn't seen since 1965—a two-barrel carburetor and single exhaust, the latter equipment shared by both SS 350s. Advertised at twenty-five more horses, the L48 350 had an 8.5:1 compression ratio as well, but was fed by a four-barrel carb. Prices were $26.90 for the L65, $75.35 for the L48. For another $101.15, a customer could have added the 300hp LS3 402 big-block, a V-8 also available throughout the A-body lineup. Exclu-

sive to RPO Z15 (at a cost of $285.15) was the LS5 454, which, despite a compression drop from 10.25:1 to 9:1, gained five horsepower over its 360hp forerunner in 1970, undoubtedly as part of a little image adjusting by the promotion guys. Proving that high-powered, high-priced big-blocks had yet to lose their appeal, the LS5 454 was installed in 9,502 Super Sports—Chevelle, El Camino, and Monte Carlo—for 1971.

Transmission choices varied by powerplant, with the base 245hp L65 being backed by either the Turbo Hydra-matic 350 automatic transmission or the M20 wide-ratio four-speed. L48 small-block transmission fare was the same, with the exception of the M11 three-speed manual included as basic equipment. The "special" MC1 heavy-duty three-speed manual was standard behind the LS3 big-block, while the M40 Turbo Hydra-matic 400

*Air pump emissions control systems first appeared as SS 396 equipment (on California cars) in 1966. In 1968, all manual transmission Super Sports got the RPO K19 air pump. In 1970, the Evaporative Emissions Control (EEC) system was designed to capture fuel vapors before they could escape and foul the air. Shown here is just part of the EEC plumbing for 1971 and 1972.*

and M20 four-speed waited in the wings (the close-ratio M21 four-speed was no longer available). LS5 customers chose between the Turbo Hydra-matic 400 and the M22 Rock Crusher four-speed. Standard axle ratios were 2.56:1 for the L65, 2.73:1 for the L48, and 3.31:1 for both big-blocks, with an optional 4.10:1 Positraction differential, RPO ZQ9, offered to LS5 buyers.

Performance figures for 1971 dropped right along with advertised

In Chevelle ranks, the LS5 454 remained an exclusive Super Sport power source for 1971—the LS3 402 could have been ordered on Chevelles with or without the Z15 package. Helping set the biggest big-block apart from the rest were the "SS 454" fender badges. LS5 Chevelles were the only Super Sports to carry exterior engine identification in 1971. No official breakdown by engine option is available for the 1971 Super Sport, but it is known that 3,148 LS5s were built for manual transmission applications and 12,234 for Turbo Hydra-matics. Applicable to full-sized Chevrolets, Monte Carlos, and Chevelles, these figures do not necessarily reflect the number of cars actually built.

outputs and compression ratios. *Motor Trend*'s Jim Brokaw reported a certainly sedate 17.10/80.42 ET for a 245hp 1971 Chevelle SS equipped with the Turbo Hydra-matic and optional 3.31:1 gears, while *Road Test*'s Ron Hickman ran a respectable 16.9/82 quarter-mile in an L48 Super Sport with the same drivetrain options. As a car "for family use, driving to and from work or the occasional trip," the L48 Chevelle SS impressed Hickman with its nice combination of decent performance, laudable handling, attractive styling, and excellent braking. "But if we were buying an SS to go racing," he pointed out, to no

one's surprise, "well, pass the air conditioning, tinted glass and special appearance groups. In with the 454 LS5, close-ratio 4-speed box [and] 4.10 rear end, and we think we would win our share."

*Car Craft*'s test crew did just that, taking home a trophy in American Hot Rod Association D-stock/automatic class competition. The crew had tested a 1971 SS 454 Chevelle driven by standard 3.31 gears, with the best quarter-mile run coming in at 14.35/97.08. After trading the 3.31s for a 4.10 Positraction unit, and adding headers and 7in slicks, the crew came up with a time slip that read 13.77

seconds at 100mph, leading *Car Craft*'s staff to conclude that, although there was certainly nothing wrong with high thirteens in the quarter-mile, the 1971 LS5 didn't quite cut it as a serious weekend warrior.

On the other hand, the 1971 454 Chevelle did "come into its own as a personal performance car, if there is such a thing," *Car Craft* wrote. "Its creature comforts included AM/FM stereo, tilt steering wheel, power steering, power disc brakes, electric door locks, cruise control and air conditioning. These niceties make the driver forget all about running down the GTX, GTO or Road Runner and help

him concentrate on how much pleasure driving can give."

So *that's* what Chevrolet's ad guys meant by "fun."

Power cutbacks notwithstanding, Chevrolet's 1971 Chevelle SS repeated as "best super car" in *Car and Driver*'s eighth annual Readers' Choice Poll, garnering 15.6 percent of the vote, compared to 13.6 percent for the second-place Road Runner/GTX from Plymouth. However, the car's apparent continuing popularity didn't exactly translate into sales success, as Chevelle Super Sport production dive-bombed to an all-time low of 19,293, a statistic purely indicative of the direc-

tion all Detroit's super cars were heading.

Along with those 19,293 Super Sports, Chevrolet sold another 6,727 "Heavy Chevy" Chevelles in 1971. Introduced midyear, the Heavy Chevy package, RPO YF3, was an obvious re-

*The 1971 Chevelle's large, new rear bumper made it impossible to continue another Super Sport tradition, the blacked-out tail treatment. On the other hand, "SS" identification and chrome exhaust tips remained (for big-block Super Sports); the "Band-Aid" stripes on the rear deck and hood were again optional under RPO D88.*

The faded air cleaner decal on this basically original 1971 LS5 454 should read "365hp," up five horses from the 1970 LS5's rating. Unlike the 402, the 1971 Super Sport's 454 kept its chrome dress-up pieces. Torque for the 1971 LS5 was a healthy 465lb-ft at 3200rpm.

*Opposite*
Except for a few tweaks up front, the 1972 Chevelle SS emerged nearly identical to the 1971. This 1972 Super Sport convertible is powered by a 350 small-block—again, no exterior engine identification was used for the 350s or 402s. Also made available for the Chevelle SS in 1972 was the low-performance 307ci small-block. Changes for 1972 included revised trim up front that fully surrounded the headlights and the completely blacked-out grille. Compare this to a view of the 1971 front end.

Indicative of how much "we've changed" was the 1971 Heavy Chevy Chevelle, a midyear offering that combined some of the Super Sport's image with a portion of its price tag. Not only that, but it was also not nearly as noticeable to the insurance crowd. All V-8s except the LS5 were available under the Heavy Chevy's domed hood, as was all other SS heavy-duty hardware, although piling up the options on this Chevelle would have defeated its budget-minded purpose.

114

*Using net ratings in 1972, Chevrolet engineers put the L48 Turbo Fire 350's output at 175hp, down ninety-five horses from 1971. With a two-barrel carburetor in place of the L48's four-barrel, the L65 350 rated at 165hp. The incorrect air cleaner decal appearing here is from a 1971 L65 small-block.*

sponse to changing attitudes, as well as an attempt to sell performance imagery to those who probably couldn't afford to operate or insure one of Chevrolet's few surviving super cars. RPO YF3 was nothing more than window dressing, although buyers could equip a Heavy Chevy with any V-8, from the standard Chevelle's Turbo Fire 307 to the LS3 Turbo Jet 400 (the LS5 was not available). YF3 features included the Super Sport's domed hood with tie-down pins; special body stripes; "Heavy Chevy" decals on the hood, fenders, and deck lid; black-ac-

cented grille and headlight bezels; and 14x6 Rally wheels without trim rings. Instead of $1,000, the approximate asking price for the stillborn 1971 LS6, RPO YF3 added slightly more than a hundred bucks to a 1971 Chevelle sticker. Whether that represented an attractive offer or not is your call.

As 1971 wound down, the picture became painfully clear. Lower octane fuels, higher insurance costs, tighter emissions standards, growing safety concerns—all these variables together could equal only one outcome, and the Heavy Chevy helped bring that outcome into focus. *Super Stock* magazine had made its call even before the 1971 model year had gotten underway: "The commanding lead Chevrolet once held over all other car makers in the horsepower numbers game is over, if not permanently, at least for the foreseeable future." And the end of the road for the Chevelle SS was not far off.

Of course, Chevrolet wasn't alone as far as sinking super cars were concerned. By 1972, Ford had basically given up the ghost, while Dodge and Plymouth were doing their best to hang in with Chrysler Corporation's hot little 340 small-block. Other than Mopar's 440ci V-8, a torque mill offered in very limited performance applications, Chevy's 454 stood unchallenged among surviving big-block super cars for 1972. Accordingly, the Chevelle SS still ranked as Detroit's most prominent muscle machine.

Other than restyled front marker lights and a revamped grille that incor-

*The 15in sport rims weren't the only Chevelle SS items borrowed from the Camaro. Along with a host of added-cost items shown here is the Camaro's optional four-spoke steering wheel, RPO NK4, which first appeared on Chevelle parts lists in 1971.*

porated the headlights, the 1972 Chevelle was a near-perfect copy of the previous edition. And save for a new, color-keyed left-hand sport mirror in place of the plated remote-control mirror used in 1971, RPO Z15 carried over almost identically as well. The one major difference came under the hood, where all Chevelle V-8s, including the truly mild Turbo Fire 307 small-block, were offered as Super Sport power sources in yet another dilution of the SS image. Made even less desirable from a performance fan's perspective due to Detroit's switch to net horsepower ratings, the Turbo Fire 307 two-

*Super Sport production for 1972, small-block or big-block, hardtop and convertible, rose from 1971's disappointing 19,293 total to 24,946. No breakdown is available for the different drivetrain combinations. This is a Turbo Jet 400 model.*

barrel V-8 advertised at 130hp; prior to 1972, the same engine carried an advertised output figure of 200hp.

All 1972 Chevrolet V-8s, from the 307 small-block to the LS5 454, were listed at 8.5:1 compression. Adjusted net outputs for the remaining Super Sport power options were 165 and 175hp, respectively, for the L65 and L48 350ci small-blocks, 240hp for the LS3 Turbo Jet 400, and 270 for the LS5.

The addition of the low-performance 307 small-block to the Super Sport lineup also meant a return of the venerable Powerglide automatic transmission, missing from SS options lists since 1968. Standard equipment behind the 307 and the L65 350 was a basic three-speed manual. Up the ladder a rung, the L48 small-block was backed by the M11 three-speed, which was optional for the L65, while the LS3 big-block got the heavy-duty MC1 three-speed. Turbo Hydra-matics were available for each of these engines,

*Notice the rear stabilizer bar underneath this Super Sport hardtop—at least the excellent F41 sport suspension remained a standard Chevelle SS feature for 1972, as did front disc brakes.*

while the M20 four-speed could be ordered behind all but the bottom-line 307. At the top, the SS-exclusive LS5 454 again was mated to either a Turbo Hydra-matic 400 or M22 Rock Crusher. In the rear, revised axle ratio choices for 1972 went only as low as 3.31:1, the standard gears for the LS5 and manual-trans LS3s.

Demonstrating just how tight emissions standards had become, buyers of the 1972 Chevelle SS in California could not order the 307 small-block or either of the Mk IV big-blocks, leaving only the two Turbo Fire 350s to carry on the Super Sport legacy on the West Coast. In the forty-nine other states, Chevrolet's SS 454 Chevelle did its best to go out with a bang. Accord-

120

ing to *Cars* magazine, a Turbo Hydra-
matic-equipped 1972 LS5 Chevelle
could trip the lights in a not-so-fantas-
tic 15.1 seconds, topping out at 93mph.
*Super Stock and Drag Illustrated* did
*Cars* one better in a four-speed SS
454, running the quarter in 14.76 seconds at 97.6mph. These numbers may
have paled in comparison to earlier efforts, but they looked awfully darn
good to those who probably knew this
was truly the end of the road.

Counting all five engines, Super
Sport production for 1972—Chevelle
and El Camino—rose slightly to
24,946 units, including 5,333 SS 454s.
Sales of the 1972 Heavy Chevy
model—itself carrying over in identical fashion from 1971—also went up,
hitting 9,508, probably because of RPO
YF3's availability throughout the 1972
model year as opposed to its abbreviat-
ed run in 1971. But even marginal
performance was gone by 1973, al-

though the Super Sport package and
454 big-block remained available, both
mere shadows of former renditions.
Like the Heavy Chevy of 1971-1972,
the 1973 Chevelle SS relied predomi-
nantly on imagery in place of real performance in order to turn customers'
heads.

Perhaps indicative of how far the
market had moved away from the
super car ideals of just a few years before, SS sales jumped to 28,647 for
1973, the last time RPO Z15 would be

*Even the top dog LS5 454 had lost its chrome dress-up by 1972. Maximum output was a net-rated 270hp at 4000rpm; maximum torque was 390lb-ft at 3200rpm.*

*Left*
*That tall shifter is attached to an M22 "Rock Crusher" four-speed, the only manual transmission listed for the LS5 454 in 1972, although apparently some aluminum-case M20 four-speeds were also used. Notice that this 1972 SS 454 has the optional Strato-bucket seats but not the console—the two items had been separate options since first being offered in 1966.*

*After 1972, Chevrolet's Chevelle SS continued for an additional year with totally restyled 1973 sheet metal, although imagery was all that remained. Buyers could add the optional LS4 454 Mk IV big-block, but true performance was no longer the game. Motor Trend reported a 10.5-second 0-60 time for an LS4-equipped 1973 Laguna sport coupe.*

offered to Chevelle buyers. Two years later, Chevrolet's 454 big-block made its final appearance as an optional intermediate model power source. El Camino Super Sports continued on, but 1973 was the end for the Chevelle SS, and rightly so. In their day, the mid-sized Super Sports were kings of the hill—to drag that high-performance image down into the no-performance seventies would have been a sin. Nearly ten years and more than 550,000 cars after it began, the Chevelle Super Sport legacy had come to a close.

*With the SS Chevelles gone, Chevrolet introduced the Type S-3 coupe for the Laguna line in 1974. Picking up where the Super Sports left off with flashy imagery inside and out and a sport suspension as standard equipment, the S-3 was nonetheless all show and no go. After 1975, it, too, expired.*

# Appendices

## *Specs & Stats*

### *Super Sport Production Figures*

**1964**

| | |
|---|---:|
| 6-cylinder convertible | 1,551 |
| 6-cylinder hardtops | 8,224 |
| **Total 6-cylinders** | **9,775** |
| | |
| V-8 convertibles | 9,640 |
| V-8 hardtops | 57,445 |
| **Total V-8s** | **67,085** |
| **Total, all 1964 Super Sports** | **76,860** |

**1965**

| | |
|---|---:|
| 6-cylinder convertible | 1,133 |
| 6-cylinder hardtops | 7,452 |
| **Total 6-cylinders** | **8,585** |
| | |
| V-8 convertibles | 7,995 |
| V-8 hardtops | 64,532 |
| **Total V-8s** | **72,527** |
| **Total all Super Sports** | **81,112** |

**Other totals:**

| | |
|---|---:|
| RPO Z16, Malibu SS 396* | 201 |

*\* includes one convertible; all others hardtops*

**1966**

| | |
|---|---:|
| SS 396 convertibles | 5,429 |
| SS 396 hardtops | 66,843 |
| **Total SS 396s, all engines** | **72,272** |

**Other totals:**

| | |
|---|---:|
| RPO L35 (325hp) 396 Custom El Caminos | |
| 1,865 | |
| RPO L34 (360hp) 396 V-8[1] | 24,811 |
| RPO L78 (375hp) 396 V-8[1] | 3,099 |
| RPO M22 four-speed transmission[2] | 12 |

[1]*For SS 396 and Custom El Camino models only*
[2]*For RPO L78 V-8 only*

## 1967

| | |
|---|---|
| SS 396 convertibles | 3,321 |
| SS 396 hardtops | 59,685 |
| **Total SS 396s, all engines** | **63,006** |

**Other totals:**

| | |
|---|---|
| RPO L35 (325hp) 396 Custom El Caminos | 2,565 |
| RPO L34 (350hp) 396 V-8[1] | 17,176 |
| RPO L78 (375hp) 396 V-8[1] | 612 |

[1] For SS 396 and Custom El Camino models only

## 1968

| | |
|---|---|
| SS 396 convertibles | 2,286 |
| SS 396 hardtops | 55,309 |
| SS 396 El Caminos | 5,190 |
| **Total SS 396s, all engines** | **62,785** |

**Other totals:**

| | |
|---|---|
| RPO L34 (360hp) 396 V-8[1] | 12,481 |
| RPO L78 (375hp) 396 V-8[1] | 4,751 |
| RPO M22 four-speed transmission[2] | 1,049 |

[1] For both SS 396 and El Camino SS 396
[2] For RPO L78 V-8 only

## 1969

| | |
|---|---|
| RPO Z25* coupes, convertibles, and El Caminos | 86,307 |

*also includes 300-series models

**Other totals:**

| | |
|---|---|
| RPO L34 (360hp) 396 V-8[1] | 17,358 |
| RPO L78 (375hp) 396 V-8[1] | 9,486 |
| RPO L89 (aluminum heads)[2] | 400 |
| RPO M22 four-speed transmission[3] | 1,276 |
| COPO 9562 427 Chevelle[4] | 373 |

[1] For both SS 396 and El Camino SS 396
[2] Should be included among L78 396 total
[3] For RPO L78 V-8 only
[4] This figure represents total number of engines built for four-speed and automatic applications; actual model production was lower, estimated at 323—ninety-nine of those were Yenko Sportscar conversions

## 1970

| | |
|---|---|
| RPO Z25 (SS 396), coupes, convertibles, & El Caminos | 53,599 |
| RPO Z15 (SS 454), coupes, convertibles, & El Caminos | 8,773 |
| **Total Super Sports, all engines** | **62,372** |

**Other totals:**

| | |
|---|---|
| RPO L34 (350hp) 396 V-8* | 51,437 |
| RPO L78 (375hp) 396 V-8* | 2,144 |
| RPO L89 (aluminum heads for L78) | 18 |
| RPO M22 four-speed transmission | 5,410 |
| RPO LS5 (360hp 454)* | 4,298 |
| RPO LS6 (450hp 454)* | 4,475 |

*For both SS 396 and El Camino SS 396

## 1971

| | |
|---|---|
| RPO Z15, coupes, convertibles, & El Caminos* | 19,293 |

*all engines, small-block and big-block

## 1972

| | |
|---|---|
| RPO Z15, coupes, convertibles, & El Caminos* | 24,946 |

*all engines, small-block and big-block

# Super Sport Engine Specifications

| RPO | CI | Horsepower | Torque | Comp. |
|---|---|---|---|---|
| **1964** | | | | |
| Std. | 194* | 120 @ 4400rpm | 177 @ 2400rpm | 8.5:1 |
| L61 | 230* | 155 @ 4400rpm | 215 @ 2000rpm | 8.5:1 |
| Std. | 283 | 195 @ 4800rpm | 285 @ 2400rpm | 9.25:1 |
| L77 | 283 | 220 @ 4800rpm | 295 @ 3200rpm | 9.25:1 |
| L30 | 327 | 250 @ 4400rpm | 350 @ 2800rpm | 10.5:1 |
| L74 | 327 | 300 @ 5000rpm | 360 @ 3200rpm | 10.5:1 |
| L76 | 327• | 365 @ 6200rpm | 350 @ 4000rpm | 11.0:1 |

\* Six-cylinders
• The L76 Corvette 327 V-8 was briefly offered; very few were built

| RPO | CI | Horsepower | Torque | Comp. |
|---|---|---|---|---|
| **1965** | | | | |
| Std. | 194* | 120 @ 4400rpm | 177 @ 2400rpm | 8.5:1 |
| L61 | 230* | 140 @ 4400rpm | 220 @ 1600rpm | 8.5:1 |
| Std. | 283 | 195 @ 4800rpm | 285 @ 2400rpm | 9.25:1 |
| L77 | 283 | 220 @ 4800rpm | 295 @ 3200rpm | 9.25:1 |
| L30 | 327 | 250 @ 4400rpm | 350 @ 2800rpm | 10.5:1 |
| L74 | 327 | 300 @ 5000rpm | 360 @ 3200rpm | 10.5:1 |
| L79 | 327 | 350 @ 5800rpm | 360 @ 3600rpm | 11.0:1 |
| L37 | 396• | 375 @ 5600rpm | 420 @ 3600rpm | 11.0:1 |

\* Six-cylinders
• Standard along with RPO Z16; only 201 were built

| RPO | CI | Horsepower | Torque | Comp. |
|---|---|---|---|---|
| **1966** | | | | |
| Std. | 396* | 325 @ 4800rpm | 410 @ 3200rpm | 10.25:1 |
| L34 | 396 | 360 @ 5200rpm | 420 @ 3600rpm | 10.25:1 |
| L78 | 396 | 375 @ 5600rpm | 415 @ 3600rpm | 11.0:1 |

\* Listed as RPO L35, Custom El Camino option
**Note:** Standard 325hp 396 had two-bolt main bearing caps; L34 and L78 had four-bolt mains

| RPO | CI | Horsepower | Torque | Comp. |
|---|---|---|---|---|
| **1967** | | | | |
| Std. | 396* | 325 @ 4800rpm | 410 @ 3200rpm | 10.25:1 |
| L34 | 396 | 350 @ 5200rpm | 415 @ 3200rpm | 10.25:1 |
| L78 | 396 | 375 @ 5600rpm | 415 @ 3600rpm | 11.0:1 |

\* Listed as RPO L35, Custom El Camino option
**Note:** Standard 325hp 396 had two-bolt main bearing caps; L34 and L78 had four-bolt mains

| RPO | CI | Horsepower | Torque | Comp. |
|---|---|---|---|---|
| **1968** | | | | |
| Std. | 396 | 325 @ 4800rpm | 410 @ 3200rpm | 10.25:1 |
| L34 | 396 | 350 @ 5200rpm | 415 @ 3200rpm | 10.25:1 |
| L78 | 396 | 375 @ 5600rpm | 415 @ 3600rpm | 11.0:1 |

**Note:** Standard 325hp 396 had two-bolt main bearing caps; L34 and L78 had four-bolt mains

| RPO | CI | Horsepower | Torque | Comp. |
|---|---|---|---|---|
| **1969** | | | | |
| L35 | 396* | 325 @ 4800rpm | 410 @ 3200rpm | 10.25:1 |
| L34 | 396 | 350 @ 5200rpm | 415 @ 3200rpm | 10.25:1 |
| L78 | 396 | 375 @ 5600rpm | 415 @ 3600rpm | 11.0:1 |
| L72 | 427 | 425 @ 5600rpm | 460 @ 4000rpm | 11.0:1 |

*\* Included with RPO Z25, the SS 396 package for Malibu, 300 Deluxe, and Custom El Camino models*
***Note 1:** Standard 325hp 396 had two-bolt main bearing caps; L34 and L78 had four-bolt mains*
***Note 2:** The 396ci Mk IV big-block was overbored to 402ci very later in the model run*
***Note 3:** RPO L89 added aluminum heads to the 375hp L78 with no change in advertised outputs*
***Note 4:** RPO L72 was Corvette V-8 used as part of the COPO 9562 High Performance Unit*

## 1970

| | | | | |
|---|---|---|---|---|
| L34 | 402* | 350 @ 5200rpm | 415 @ 3400rpm | 10.25:1 |
| L78 | 402 | 375 @ 5600rpm | 415 @ 3600rpm | 11.0:1 |
| LS5 | 454• | 360 @ 5400rpm | 500 @ 3200rpm | 10.25:1 |
| LS6 | 454 | 450 @ 5600rpm | 500 @ 3600rpm | 11.25:1 |

*\* Included with RPO Z25, the SS 396 package for Malibu hardtops and convertibles and Custom El Caminos*
*• Included with RPO Z15, the SS 454 package for Malibu hardtops and convertibles and Custom El Caminos*
***Note 1:** L34 and L78 V-8s were referred to still as Turbo-Jet 396s despite the slight increase in displacement*
***Note 2:** The LS5 454 had two-bolt main bearing caps; the LS6 had four-bolt mains*
***Note 3:** RPO L89 added aluminum heads to the 375hp L78 with no change in advertised outputs; RPO L89 was cancelled early in the model run (only 18 were built)*

## 1971

| | | | | |
|---|---|---|---|---|
| L65* | 350 | 245 @ 4800rpm | 350 @ 2800rpm | 8.5:1 |
| L48 | 350 | 270 @ 4800rpm | 360 @ 3200rpm | 8.5:1 |
| LS3• | 402 | 300 @ 4800rpm | 400 @ 3200rpm | 8.5:1 |
| LS5 | 454 | 365 @ 4800rpm | 465 @ 3200rpm | 8.5:1 |

*\* Had two-barrel carburetor; L48 had four-barrel*
*• Identified as the Turbo-Jet 400*
***Note 1:** All engines, small-block or big-block, were offered as part of RPO Z15, the SS package for Malibu hardtops and convertibles and Custom El Caminos*
***Note 2:** Both small-block V-8s, L65 and L48, had single exhausts*
***Note 3:** The LS5 454 had two-bolt main bearing caps; the LS6 had four-bolt mains*
***Note 4:** Only the LS5 SS 454 Chevelle carried external identification—all other Super Sports, big-block or small-block, were simply labeled "SS"*

## 1972

| | | | | |
|---|---|---|---|---|
| Std.* | 307 | 130 @ 4000rpm | 230 @ 2400rpm | 8.5:1 |
| L65* | 350 | 165 @ 4000rpm | 280 @ 2400rpm | 8.5:1 |
| L48 | 350 | 175 @ 4000rpm | 280 @ 2400rpm | 8.5:1 |
| LS3• | 402 | 240 @ 4400rpm | 345 @ 3200rpm | 8.5:1 |
| LS5 | 454 | 270 @ 4000rpm | 390 @ 3200rpm | 8.5:1 |

*\* Had two-barrel carburetor; L48 had four-barrel*
*• Identified as the Turbo-Jet 400*
***Note 1:** All engines, small-block or big-block, were offered as part of RPO Z15, the SS package for Malibu hardtops and convertibles and Custom El Caminos*
***Note 2:** All three small-block V-8s, Standard 307, L65, and L48, had single exhausts*
***Note 3:** Only the LS5 SS 454 Chevelle carried external identification—all other Super Sports, big-block or small-block, were simply labeled "SS"*

## 1973

| | | | | |
|---|---|---|---|---|
| L65* | 350 | 145 @ 4000rpm | 255 @ 2400rpm | 8.5:1 |
| L48 | 350 | 175 @ 4000rpm | 260 @ 2800rpm | 8.5:1 |
| LS4 | 454 | 245 @ 4000rpm | 375 @ 2800rpm | 8.5:1 |

*\* Had two-barrel carburetor; L48 had four-barrel*
***Note 1:** All engines, small-block or big-block, were offered as part of RPO Z15, the SS package for Malibu Colonade coupes and Malibu station wagons.*

# Index